EXECUTIVE LEADERSHIP IN NONPROFIT ORGANIZATIONS

Robert D. Herman
Richard D. Heimovics

●●●

EXECUTIVE LEADERSHIP IN NONPROFIT ORGANIZATIONS

●●

New Strategies for Shaping Executive–Board Dynamics

Jossey-Bass Publishers

San Francisco • Oxford • 1991

EXECUTIVE LEADERSHIP IN NONPROFIT ORGANIZATIONS
New Strategies for Shaping Executive-Board Dynamics
by Robert D. Herman and Richard D. Heimovics

Library of Congress Cataloging-in-Publication Data

Herman, Robert D., date.
    Executive leadership in nonprofit organizations : new strategies
for shaping executive-board dynamics / Robert D. Herman, Richard D.
Heimovics. — 1st ed.
        p.   cm. — (The Jossey-Bass nonprofit sector series)
    Includes bibliographical references and index.
    ISBN 1-55542-334-5 (alk. paper)
    1. Corporations, Nonprofit — Management.   I. Heimovics, Richard, date.
II. Title.   III. Series.
HD62.6.H47   1991
658.4'092 — dc20   90-21028
                                                                    CIP

Manufactured in the United States of America

The paper in this book meets the guidelines for
permanence and durability of the Committee on
Production Guidelines for Book Longevity of
the Council on Library Resources.

JACKET DESIGN BY WILLI BAUM

FIRST EDITION

Code 9137

The Jossey-Bass
Nonprofit Sector Series

○○○

CONTENTS

●●●

PREFACE

●●●

I work for the board. It's not my responsibility to lead them. They have to lead themselves.

The board thinks I work for them. I know how to make them happy. I give them nice-looking reports, no problems, and lots of recognition. I keep them from messing things up.

Sure, I work for the board. But we all work for the kids. My job is to see that we — me, the board, everybody — work together to do what's right for the kids.

These statements illustrate the range of ways that nonprofit chief executives conceptualize their leadership role in relation to their boards of directors. They are derived from our empirical study of nonprofit executives, which in turn provides the basis for this book. We found that some executives hold fast to a traditional hierarchical model in which they see themselves as subordinate in all ways to the board. Such a view means that when the board fails to carry out its self-defined duties, the chief executive can do nothing but ask it to do better. Other executives develop a more cynical, manipulative approach. They act as if the board is in charge, but structure activities so that the board merely rat-

ifies their decisions. The board, indeed, becomes the proverbial rubber stamp.

A last group of executives enact the model on which this
book is based. These executives, whom our research discovered
to be especially effective, have found that they can get more done
for the organization and its mission if they take responsibility
for aiding the board in fulfilling its obligations. They do this
by regarding their boards as fundamental to the organization's
mission. They have discovered ways of energizing and focusing their boards. In short, they have resolved the longstanding
disjunction between the leadership centrality of the chief executive and the formal, hierarchical superiority of the board.

Abundant evidence testifies to the difficulties nonprofit
boards often have in meeting the expectations assigned them
under the traditional model. The National Center for Nonprofit
Boards, which was established in 1988 to "improve the effectiveness of nonprofit organizations by strengthening their boards
of directors," offers a variety of publications about boards and
helps design and conduct board development programs. Books
and articles providing advice on how boards can more effectively meet their obligations appear with ever-increasing frequency. In communities across the country an increasing number of programs and workshops on board development are being
offered. Clearly, there is a problem with the performance of
boards — one that affects the performance of both chief executives and their boards. However, we believe the board problem is really a nonprofit organization problem that stems from
an inadequate understanding of the unique character of nonprofit organizations and their leadership requirements.

Nonprofit chief executives have for too long been captives
of a hierarchical model of organizations that places the board
at the top of the chain of authority and responsibility and at
the center of leadership in nonprofit organizations. Executives
in these organizations have needed an alternative conception —
one that corresponds to the operational reality. Such a conception would provide a more useful basis for working with the
board.

The purpose of this book is to delineate this alternative

conception. We describe the unique character and realities of nonprofit organizations and contrast the traditional hierarchical model and its role prescriptions with our more realistic alternative. The alternative model is based on our recent research and details the leadership behaviors of effective nonprofit chief executives. In particular, the alternative model emphasizes that effective chief executives often must take responsibility for clarifying and acting to advance the board's role. If a nonprofit organization is to be effective, it is usually the chief executive who must engage the board in clarifying their respective and mutually shared roles and responsibilities in the organizational leadership process.

This book differs from others on nonprofit management and leadership in two ways. First, we focus on the chief executive's role. No other book gives detailed attention to the central leadership responsibility of the chief executive. Our research shows that board members and staff expect chief executives to take responsibility for success and failure and that they do take such responsibility. Thus, we argue, the board's performance becomes the executive's responsibility. We can no longer expect boards, in most cases, to improve their performance independently. Drawing on the experience of especially effective executives, we provide guidance on the ways executives can get things done in their communities, working with and through their boards.

Second, as we focus on the leadership role of the chief executive, we also consider the roles and responsibilities of boards. However, in doing so we do not treat boards in isolation from the rest of the organization. Board performance can only be understood and improved in relation to the rest of the organization. In particular, we emphasize what boards do — and should — expect from chief executives.

Who Should Read This Book

We believe this book will be especially useful for two sets of people. We directly address practicing nonprofit chief executives. We especially hope that those chief executives who have felt that there must be a better way to work with their boards will find these ideas helpful. We believe we offer a useful model of executive leadership that identifies a number of specific behaviors that can be developed and applied in many different situations.

We also believe that senior managers who aspire to become chief executives will find the book useful. Such managers will, in most cases, have had some experience in working with boards and observing others working with boards. Such lessons of experience are undoubtedly beneficial, but often we learn from experience only what we are prepared to learn. Thus, we anticipate that senior managers will benefit from a new way of thinking about the board-executive relationship. They will be better prepared to quickly develop effective relationships with their first boards if they have learned the lessons we have drawn from the experience of especially effective executives.

We think this book can be useful for other groups besides current and prospective chief executives. Board members — particularly those interested in finding a better way of relating to their chief executives — will find that our model respects the crucial role of the board. In addition, by legitimating the leadership centrality of chief executives, it enables boards to more easily meet their responsibilities. We also expect the book to be of value to the growing number of students pursuing courses in nonprofit organization management, voluntarism, and philanthropy. Such students are, of course, frequently part of one of the other potential audiences. However, even those students who are not now executives, staff, or board members will, we believe, learn much here about the practice of effective executive leadership.

Overview of the Contents

In the first three chapters of this book we describe and analyze the unique environmental (that is, the legal, political, economic, and philanthropic) context of nonprofit organizations. We also examine the ways this context affects the nature of nonprofit organizations and their leadership.

Chapter One describes the complex environment in which nonprofit organizations operate. We illustrate that complexity with composite case studies drawn from our research, giving special attention to the impact of environmental changes in the last decade on nonprofit organization leadership. We identify the two major leadership challenges as developing financial resources and managing the board-executive relationship.

In Chapter Two we examine how the unique characteristics and increasing complexity of the environment affect nonprofit organizations. Because nonprofit organizations are especially open (that is, affected by their environments) and dependent on external resources, leadership requires constant interaction with the surrounding environment, as well as entrepreneurial and political skills.

Chapter Three confronts the troubling issues of authority, responsibility, and leadership. In this chapter we first describe the managed systems model of nonprofit organizations. This traditional model places the board at the top of the hierarchy and at the center of leadership. We think this view incomplete and the source of many leadership breakdowns. We draw on our own research and that of others to develop an alternative model. This alternative is based on two key empirical results: (1) chief executives are expected to and do carry out the central leadership role, and (2) especially effective chief executives combine this central leadership position with highly developed skills in board leadership. We examine the implications of the alternative model for the standards we should hold regarding leadership and management of nonprofit organizations.

The final three chapters are devoted to considering the practical implications of our alternative model of leadership. In these chapters we suggest how chief executives can more effectively meet the challenges their organizations face. In Chapter Four we specify the implications of our leadership model for understanding and influencing the external environment. We describe and illustrate the strategies effective executives have used to position their organizations for increased support.

Chapter Five provides detailed guidance for executives committed to improving their effectiveness in working with their boards. We emphasize the necessity of diagnosing causes of inadequate board performance and of practicing collaborative skills as executive and board enhance their mutual effectiveness. We give particular attention to the importance of the mission and of exchange processes as bases for developing effective boards and discuss useful ways of recruiting and orienting new board members.

Chapter Six argues that effective chief executives meet the challenges of developing financial resources and managing executive-board relations by working with and through the board to position their organizations in the changing environment. Here we describe six specific board leadership skills in detail and offer suggestions for executives to assess the extent to which they are practicing such board-centered leadership. We also suggest ways in which executives might further develop these skills.

In the Afterword we highlight the main themes of the book and encourage chief executives to accept the challenge of leadership centrality. A resources section provides guidelines and work sheets that could be used, in a board retreat or some similar occasion, to help an executive and the board open discussion about the leadership function and reach clarification about how they want to work with each other.

Acknowledgments

We have benefited substantially from the help and advice of others. The research on which this book is based was funded by a grant from the University of Missouri's Weldon Springs Endowment Fund. We are grateful for that support. We also received funding from the Beistle Memorial fund of the Cookingham Institute of Public Affairs of the Bloch School of Business and Public Administration at the University of Missouri, Kansas City. We thank our colleagues for that. Of course, the research was possible only because of the extensive and patient cooperation of all the chief executives, staff, and board members who talked with our interviewers and returned our questionnaires. We are very grateful for their help in this project and for their support more generally. We also wish to acknowledge the work of those who participated in the project as interviewers, ratings judges, coders, and research assistants: Barbara Britt, Carol

Evans, Bill Grotts, Cathy Heimovics, Barbara O'Hearn, Anne Rudigier, and Mark Thoma-Perry.

We appreciate the helpful conversations we have had with Melissa Middleton Stone. Her analysis of the authority and responsibility relations between chief executives and boards has substantially informed our research and this book. Many of our colleagues have discussed with us the issues we consider here and given us the benefit of their criticisms of drafts of this book. We very much appreciate the help of Beth Smith, Ed Weaver, Rick Malsick, and Barbara Wilkerson. We also appreciate the comments of three anonymous reviewers, as well as the helpful advice and support of Alan Shrader, our editor at Jossey-Bass. Special thanks to Lauretha Cobb for her work in producing several early drafts and this final manuscript. Finally, our deepest appreciation to Charlotte Herman and Cathy Heimovics.

Kansas City, Missouri   Robert D. Herman
January 1991   Richard D. Heimovics

THE AUTHORS

○○

Robert D. Herman is professor of organizational behavior and community psychology at the University of Missouri, Kansas City, where he teaches in the nonprofit management program of the Cookingham Institute of Public Affairs in the Henry W. Bloch School of Business and Public Administration. He received his B.A. degree (1968) from Kansas State University in economics and both his M.S. (1971) and Ph.D. (1976) degrees from Cornell University in organizational behavior.

Herman's chief research interests have been voluntary behavior and nonprofit organizations, with particular attention to executive leadership, governance, and effectiveness. He is senior editor, with Jon Van Til, of *Nonprofit Boards of Directors: Analyses and Applications* (1989). He has published more than forty articles and book chapters. Recent articles have appeared in the *Journal of Voluntary Action Research, Nonprofit and Voluntary Sector Quarterly, Humanity and Society, Journal of Sociology and Social Welfare, Sex Roles, American Review of Public Administration,* and *Nonprofit Management and Leadership.*

Herman is past president (1988–1990) of the Association of Voluntary Action Scholars (now known as the Association for Research on Nonprofit Organizations and Voluntary Action) and was formerly president of a nonprofit charitable organization, in addition to other nonprofit board service.

Richard D. Heimovics is professor of organizational behavior at the Cookingham Institute of Public Affairs in the Henry W. Bloch School of Business and Public Administration at the University of Missouri, Kansas City, where he teaches students of business management, public management, and nonprofit management. He received his A.B. degree (1963) from Dartmouth College in history, his M.P.A. degree (1969) from the University of Missouri, Kansas City, in public administration, and his Ph.D. degree (1975) from the University of Kansas in human relations and communications.

Heimovics's main research activities recently have been in leadership and management of nonprofit organizations. He has also studied and written about work group performance and organizational change, management in the public sector, education for public service, and research and development in universities.

He is coeditor of two books and author of thirty-five publications and serves on the editorial board of two academic journals. His research has been reported in the *Journal of Voluntary Action Research, Nonprofit and Voluntary Sector Quarterly, Southern Review of Public Administration, Midwest Review of Public Administration, American Review of Public Administration, Sex Roles, Nonprofit Management and Leadership, Educational Administration Quarterly,* and *Small Group Behavior.*

Heimovics is past president of the National Association of Schools of Public Affairs and Administration (1986–1987), where he was responsible for encouraging research in and the study of nonprofit organizations in the schools of public affairs and administration.

EXECUTIVE LEADERSHIP IN NONPROFIT ORGANIZATIONS

•••

ONE

New Challenges
for Nonprofit Executives

ooooooooooooooooooooooooooooooooooooooooooooooo

Increasingly, the large numbers of organizations belonging to what is known variously as the "nonprofit," "voluntary," "charitable," or "third" sector are called upon to play a major role in determining the overall quality of American life. Despite the long history and substantial importance of voluntarism, philanthropy, and nonprofit organizations in our society, only recently have these organizations been the subject of much study. Over the last decade, research on a number of issues related to the nonprofit sector has been rapidly expanding (for example, Galaskiewicz, 1985; Hodgkinson and Lyman, 1989; Odendahl, 1987; O'Neill, 1989; Powell, 1987; Van Til, 1988). Although we are beginning to understand the profound roles such institutions play in the lives of most people, it is surprising how little is known about the actions and strategies of those who lead these organizations.

However, as we have come to understand more about the nonprofit sector and its voluntaristic and philanthropic roots, we are beginning to understand the special challenges faced by the leadership of these organizations. The aim of this book is to describe and enhance the skills of effective leaders in nonprofit organizations. We begin by identifying and describing the two major leadership challenges for those who aspire to

1

strengthen the nonprofit sector in our pluralist society: finding financial resources, and clarifying the responsibilities of the board and the chief executive.

Finding Financial Resources

There are three major sources of funds to operate nonprofit organizations: governmental funding through contracts and grants, sales of services or goods in the marketplace, and donations from individuals, foundations, and corporations. Options for revenue generation are thus actually broader in the nonprofit sector than in business or government. However, it is becoming increasingly difficult to gain financial resources from all of these potential sources.

Historically, government at all levels has provided major funding for many of the activities pursued by nonprofit organizations. As federal policymakers have begun to focus on reducing the federal deficit and federal support has been dramatically scaled back, state and local governments and the private sector have been expected to take up the slack. This expectation is unlikely to change in the 1990s as a continuing federal deficit makes future declines in federal funding even more likely.

Simultaneously, direct service provision by government is being reduced in many fields. Although state and local governments have stepped in to make up some of the loss in federal funding, and private giving has increased, state and local governments are hard-pressed to make up the difference because of their own financial constraints. Corporations, foundations, and individual givers cannot substitute for public-sector funding. Burgeoning social ills compound the problem as nonprofit organizations are increasingly expected to care for persons with AIDS, help drug abusers and educate for drug use prevention, feed and house the poor, assist the elderly, teach the illiterate, and otherwise compensate for failing educational and social systems. As a result of these factors, the most fundamental problem facing many of the leaders of nonprofit organizations is the continuing effort needed to find and sustain financial resources sufficient to carry out the mission of the organization during a time of declining government support and intensifying competition for available funds.

Most nonprofit organizations also sell their services in the marketplace, behaving similarly to profit-seeking businesses. The marketing strategies of many nonprofit organizations often look very similar to those in the private sector. Borrowed capital investments and revenues from sales of goods and services provide the funds necessary for profit-seeking organizations to compete in the marketplace. Such a business must measure up to the bottom line. A nonprofit organization must also meet a bottom-line measure — that of at least breaking even. A well-managed nonprofit organization will often achieve some (small) surplus, but the extent of the surplus does not provide a useful measure of success.

The nonprofit executive leader must also take another kind of bottom line into consideration. Governmental funding decisions for nonprofit organizations are made in the political arena in the context of taxation and allocation authority and competing claims about the public interest. The successful nonprofit executive leader who seeks public dollars must be proficient in this political marketplace.

The third major source of funds for most nonprofit organizations is charitable giving. Significant resources are often obtained in this arena.

The skills and strategies important for succeeding in each of these arenas are in some ways quite different from each other. The executive leadership challenge involves orchestrating an effective strategy for obtaining the appropriate mix of sources for the particular organization. The difficulty of integrating the different approaches is illustrated in the case studies of two typical nonprofit organizations given in this chapter. The events are drawn from our research interviews with nonprofit chief executives, board members, and other staff. Although the context of the events is the field of social and mental health services, the problems faced by Joe Brown, executive director of the Northwest Neighborhood Center in Anytown, U.S.A., and his good friend Alice Berger, president of the Nielson Home, are conceptually identical with those in other kinds of organizations.

(The names and characteristics of the people and organizations described here have been disguised to preserve anonymity.)

Joe Brown and the Northwest Neighborhood Center

For decades the Northwest Neighborhood Center has offered a variety of programs for its community: day care for infants and the elderly, home improvement and rehabilitation loan programs, recreation activities, and many other social and human services. One of the most successful programs was now in trouble. Joe Brown, the executive director of the center, read the letter again. The bad news had not improved after a second reading. Even though he had some reason to expect the disturbing message, it was still hard to accept. State funds for the highly successful teenage drug treatment program at the center were about to be cut. The center would be offered a contract from the state Department of Human Services at a daily rate lower than last year, and last year's program did not break even.

The cut was serious, weakening one of the center's best programs. The treatment efforts had been extremely well received in the community. A recent editorial in the local newspaper praised the program, giving the center solid publicity for its innovative efforts. The program was well managed; a program evaluation of last year's activities had demonstrated that it was cost effective by every measure. For these and other reasons and because of his own belief in the importance of the program, Joe had remained optimistic about improved state funding despite rumors that problems for the program were brewing in the state capital.

The drug treatment program was part of a citywide, coordinated effort among a number of agencies, including the center. The activities of the center were directed at teenagers who were in the last stages of recovery. Efforts were aimed at activities to help these teenagers move back into their community to live a drug-free life. The center provided support programs for specially designated teenagers recently released from inpatient, extended-care drug treatment facilities in Anytown. One of these clinics was managed by his good friend Alice Berger, president of the Nielson Home. Joe made a mental note that he would have to talk with her soon about the possible implications of the cut for the contract between the center and the home.

Joe had learned a lot about drug treatment in the past few years. Help for teenagers is most successful when there is a comprehensive effort based on cooperation among many agencies, inpatient and outpatient facilities, and programs like those at the center. Counseling, support groups, education, and physical fitness were the center's contributions to a comprehensive system of care. Joe feared that the system would begin to unravel without the center's efforts. It had taken Joe, his staff, and the community three years to get the system running smoothly. The impending cuts meant that carefully negotiated relations among the different agencies would begin to break down. Dedicated staff would have to be released. More importantly, teenagers who desperately needed the kind of programs the center offered would be left to their own devices. Without the support services of the center, many would revert to the lives they knew before treatment.

Joe had been communicating this possibility to the center's board of directors for some months, and the board's planning committee had suggested that the center seek foundation and/or corporate support in the event that state funding was cut back. Using gift funds was a possibility, but Joe did not want to siphon off charitable funds needed for other programs offered by the center. He knew that the fund-raising committee would be reluctant to add this program to its fund-raising efforts, which were already well under way. On the other hand, a majority of the board had a strong investment in the drug program and expected Joe to present a workable alternative at all costs. Another group of board members believed the center should raise fees in general for those services it provided. The bad news in the letter would just complicate decisions about new funding strategies. The letter Joe held in his hand was brief, but the implications for the center and Anytown were far-reaching.

The Northwest Neighborhood Center and many thousands of similar organizations are part of a unique system that includes funders, regulators, beneficiaries, support organizations, and other nonprofit organizations and clients. The interactions among the parts of this system influence the resource bases of nonprofit organizations and create special problems for the executive leadership of these organizations. To understand what constitutes effective leadership of these organizations, one needs to examine how the chief executive and the volunteer boards of these organizations respond to this system.

Clarifying Responsibilities Between the Volunteer Board and the Chief Executive

The relationship between the volunteer board of directors and the chief executive of the nonprofit organization constitutes the second unique leadership challenge. From Joe's perspective, the issue of the board's role in solving the funding problem raises questions generically similar to those facing countless other nonprofit executives, and the answers are seldom, if ever, conclusive. One of the most pressing concerns is the division of responsibility between Joe and his board.

The structure of nonprofit organizations substantively affects leadership roles and complicates the processes of decision making. Moreover, there is an important difference between statements about how this relationship is supposed to operate and how it actually works. The Northwest Neighborhood Center, like all nonprofit organizations, has a board of directors presumed to be at the helm. This board, comprised of citizen volunteers, is assumed to reflect the interests and needs of Anytown. It is expected that Joe works at the board's pleasure, and it is to the board that Joe is responsible for the services and activities of the Northwest Neighborhood Center. The volunteer board is expected to be in charge of the activities of the center. It is expected to establish policy, plan for the future, oversee programs, and develop standards to ensure accomplishment of the organization's mission.

The relationship between chief executives and boards is legally and in some ways practically that of superior to subordinate. But Joe knows that the relationship is always more complex than that. Ideally, it is characterized by trust and collaboration in which the parties bring complementary skills and perspectives to their joint work. The fact that the organizational relationship is both hierarchical and lateral makes it one in which it is a challenge to find effective ways of working together.

There are a number of other reasons for the complex relationship. First, successful chief executives like Joe often have much better information about the organization, its funding sources, and its problems in program delivery than do most board members, and Joe can often make more informed decisions about the activities of his organization. Although the board is the legal and hierarchical superior, it is usually very dependent on the chief executive for information and expertise.

Second, board members like those at the Northwest Neighborhood Center may feel varying degrees of stake in the many programs. The drug treatment program is only one of many programs at the center. Board members cannot be expected to understand or address all the problems affecting every program or activity of the center. In all nonprofit organizations, the levels of commitment and the knowledge base of board members will vary.

Third, while board members have other major life commitments and responsibilities, the chief executive role is commonly the central part of the executive's life. It is Joe's job and career. The board works on a volunteer basis, which means there will be various levels of commitment among board members to work on problems. Joe does not have to choose between obligations at the center and obligations at another job, as do most board members.

Fourth, the programs of nonprofit organizations like the center are often the result of the organization taking advantage of opportunities found in the social and political fabric of the community rather than the result of careful strategic planning by the board. Joe is often engaged in scouting missions in the community looking for program and funding opportunities. In other words, funding opportunities beget programs, and Joe is expected to be on the lookout for new program dollars. When funding for the drug program became available, it seemed to fit the mission of the center and the needs of the neighborhood. Until funding was secured, however, teenage drug treatment was not a priority for some members of the board. Success and publicity later made the program one that the board as a whole embraced. Despite its high priority with his board, Joe was soon to discover why the program was receiving a much lower priority at the state capital.

> As Joe drove to the state capital to inquire about the reasons for the cuts and to plead his case one last time, he thought about his role at the center and with the board. He had talked personally with each board member and assured them they would be kept fully informed about the impending cut. But he also knew it would be largely his responsibility to come up with a strategy to deal with the problem. The issues were terribly complex, however.
>
> The consequences of the cut would be far-reaching. The center had contracts with three inpatient drug treatment centers at local hospitals and with the Nielson Home for Children, which had recently established a drug treatment program for teenagers. New negotiations with the hospitals and the home would be necessary or contracts would be broken. How these decisions were handled would affect the future of the center and its relations with other organizations. Differences among board members about how to proceed with revising contracts were almost certain.
>
> Joe drove alone to the state capital. He was intent on finding out more about the funding crisis to see if he could do anything about it. The board president could not make the journey because of personal business, which was unfortunate for Joe, but not unexpected. The board president was a busy man, highly dedicated to the center but unable to attend all the key meetings affecting it. Joe,

nonetheless, had looked forward to the long conversations the trip would have provided. Joe was used to using the board president's time carefully. The drive would have been a good time to talk about the board's likely response to the cut.

Joe had another item of personal business to discuss with his president. More was at stake than just the continuation of a successful program. Joe had recommended to the board only nominal increases in his salary the last three years, as he concentrated salary increases on key program managers. He had planned to ask for a more substantial raise this year. But the impending cut created a delicate situation. It seemed to Joe that when the chips were down, almost everything that happened at the center affected him directly. Not only did a lot of fingers point to him as being responsible for the most crucial things that happened at the center, but the key decisions that were made always affected his job directly.

Coping with the Changing Political and Social Environment of the Nonprofit Organization

As we have seen in the case of Joe, the chief executive is faced with a major leadership challenge. The complex relations between the chief executive and the board of directors are an important element of the challenge. The executive-board relationship has been appropriately labeled "strange loops and tangled hierarchies" (Middleton, 1987, p. 149). Two opposing orientations of organizational leadership add to the entanglements between the chief executive and the board. On the one hand, an internal orientation focuses on personnel and administrative matters to achieve efficient operation and ensure the effective delivery of programs and services. It is clear to most leaders like Joe that they are held primarily responsible for these basic internal managerial activities. On the other hand, a different set of leadership tasks requires action in the external environment of the organization, where support for new programs is developed and resources found.

These actions, which span the boundary between the organization and its social, economic, and political environment, create a set of problems different from the organization's regular business of delivering services efficiently. Successful boundary-spanning leaders like Joe and his board must deal regularly with those environmental factors that affect the internal operations of the organization. Here the tangled web of responsibility between the board and Joe is most complicated. Here also the leadership of nonprofit organizations is often faced with the choice between remaining reactive to a changing external environment or engaging proactively in strategies that might shape the environment in ways favorable to the organization. The choice can often be made between maintenance behaviors and change-oriented strategies.

As we continue to trace Joe's problem with the funding cut, we realize that a resolution to the problem cannot be adequately met by trying to improve the delivery of services from the center; that is, by managing more efficiently. Improving the cost effectiveness or the quality of the services will do little to remedy things. Funding for the center's drug treatment program is determined by a political agenda much larger than the narrower issues of efficient service delivery at the community center. The issue is embedded in the politics of state government at the highest levels. To address the problem, Joe must work outside the boundaries of the center to influence decisions made far beyond the confines of Anytown.

State government had always been perplexing to Joe. He was only now beginning to understand it. At the appropriate office of the Department of Human Services, he quickly discovered the reasons for the cuts. He learned from the recently appointed director of the department that the new governor's recent drug treatment initiative was, ironically, at the source of the problem. The governor had campaigned for office on the pledge that drug treatment was to reach all parts of the state, "urban and rural, big city and small." After taking office, the governor discovered that it would require a major reallocation of the budget for the Department of Human Services to handle the increased costs of the drug program he proposed.

To complicate matters, many more applications had been received this year than last for the funds. The increasing drug crisis and heightened expectations from the publicity during the governor's campaign were believed to be the cause. At the direction of the director of the department, scarce human service dollars were now being spread even more broadly across the state for drug treatment while the governor sought more funds from the legislature. In short, the reallocation meant that money originally planned for the center was going elsewhere.

The center, heavily dependent as it was on public dollars, was constantly making adjustments and readjustments as funding priorities shifted in the political winds of the state. Joe could describe all this to his board, but it would take half a board meeting just to explain what the cuts in the drug treatment program really meant to Anytown and the center. What would be the best time, Joe wondered, to share this information with the board? One thing he knew for sure. It would be more than the board could handle at its next meeting. That agenda was full.

If only he or someone had a way to influence the funding decision at the state capital, Joe thought as he drove back to Anytown. He knew, however, that neither he nor any of those who had a stake in the center had that kind of access to power. He made a mental note that the center needed to add board members who had better political clout in the capital.

Although Joe's board was representative of the community, it was hardly an elite group. Great pains had always been taken to ensure that the board represented the diverse interests of the community. A balance was carefully maintained, taking into account age, gender, race, education, and economic standing. He knew that to diversify the membership to include the kind of heavy hitters whose voices could be heard in the state capital would certainly alter the composition of the board. It most likely would even require adding members from outside the community. The "family" would have to open itself up to potentially powerful outside interests. He knew some board members would be reluctant to go along with this strategy. His relationship with the board might be altered. Joe had always been accepted as one of the family. He would now be forced to argue for bringing outsiders onto the board.

The nonprofit organization that Joe must manage has been and continues to be shaped by changing political, economic, and social conditions not just in Anytown, not just at the state capital, but in our country at large. Figure 1 presents a schematic summary of the most important components of this system. At the center of the system is a nonprofit organization, one of many thousands like the Northwest Neighborhood Center. The figure emphasizes that a nonprofit organization interacts first of all with a near, or operating, environment—those organizations, groups, and individuals that have direct, fairly frequent, exchanges with it. These organizations, groups, and individuals are, of course, engaged in similar interactions within their own systems. Thus, factors in the larger environment affect the operating environment and its exchanges with the nonprofit organization.

The figure also emphasizes the variety of exchanges that a nonprofit organization has with other parties in its environment. Some parties are more important to the nonprofit organization as suppliers of inputs. For instance, donors or givers are often crucial for providing the funding necessary to avoid deficits. Some donors expect and demand certain outputs, such as specific programs that they have agreed to support. Donors often expect reports about the conduct of the programs in order to hold organizations accountable. Some donors, such as individuals, may demand less accountability. While regulators seldom supply funds, they can provide legitimacy (that is, approval). They can prescribe or proscribe service technologies (for example, what treatments are permitted and what prohibited for differing sorts of mental illness) and require specific outputs (for example, a staff-client ratio or a certain number of hours weekly of a particular therapy). Thus, regulators often influence

Figure 1. U.S. Philanthrophic System.

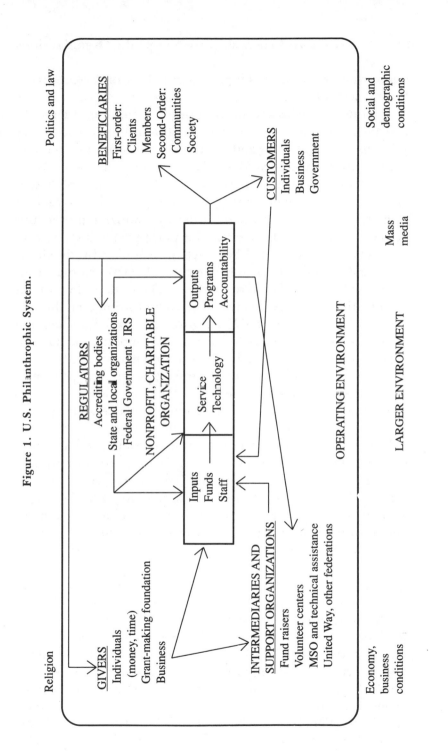

Religion

Politics and law

BENEFICIARIES
First-order:
Clients
Members
Second-Order:
Communities
Society

CUSTOMERS
Individuals
Business
Government

REGULATORS
Accrediting bodies
State and local organizations
Federal Government - IRS

NONPROFIT, CHARITABLE
ORGANIZATION

Outputs
Programs
Accountability

Service
Technology

Inputs
Funds
Staff

GIVERS
Individuals
(money, time)
Grant-making foundation
Business

INTERMEDIARIES AND
SUPPORT ORGANIZATIONS
Fund raisers
Volunteer centers
MSO and technical assistance
United Way, other federations

OPERATING ENVIRONMENT

LARGER ENVIRONMENT

Economy,
business
conditions

Mass
media

Social and
demographic
conditions

a nonprofit organization's inputs, technology or service procedures, and outputs.

Intermediaries and support organizations are those that have been created to assist nonprofit organizations or to broker relations between givers and nonprofit organizations. In many communities the United Way often functions in both capacities, at least for those organizations with which it is affiliated. The United Way may assist by providing technical assistance in the form of a Management Support Organization or volunteer center, which helps recruit and place people interested in volunteering. The United Way acts as a broker by, in effect, assuring donors that their contributions will go to well-managed, deserving health and welfare charities. The leaders of nonprofit organizations are expected to maintain and strengthen the various relationships illustrated in Figure 1, be aware of changing conditions affecting these relationships, and take actions to respond quickly and effectively to those changes.

The events affecting the Northwest Neighborhood Center have been very familiar ones over the last several years, as governmental funding for many programs carried out by nonprofit organizations has been cut while service demands grow and costs rise. The nonprofit-government relationship is generally conceived of as a partnership, with each partner dependent upon the other to varying degrees. This partnership has been subject to stresses and strains in recent years, especially with changes in the nature of support by the federal government. The constantly shifting priorities in the government's relationship with nonprofit organizations places a major burden upon that partnership.

The growing dependence of nonprofit organizations upon government funding has been carefully documented. The Urban Institute's Project on the Nonprofit Sector provided groundbreaking evidence about this relationship. In a sixteen-community study, Salamon, Musselwhite, and De Vita (1986) found that governments, at all levels, directly provide about 40 percent of the services they fund, with another 40 percent delivered by nonprofit organizations and the remaining 20 percent by business firms. The same study, which gathered data from 3,400 nonprofit organizations in the sixteen communities, also revealed that on average about 40 percent of the income of human service nonprofit organizations came from government, while 30 percent was derived from fees, 20 percent from donations, and the balance from other sources — for example, investments and so forth (Salamon, 1987). These data clearly provide evidence of the extent of dependence of many nonprofit organizations upon government dollars.

Many nonprofit organizations have increasingly found themselves making adjustments like those at the center because of this dependence. For a variety of reasons, including changing federal priorities during the 1980s, the nonprofit, charitable sector has been expected to respond (and has responded) to increased needs for services to the homeless, those on drugs, and those who are victims of domestic violence and abuse; for programs in early childhood development; for education and job training programs; and for programs in many other areas. At the same time, federal funds allocated to support nonprofit programs declined by an inflation-adjusted 22 percent between 1980 and 1988 (Salamon and Abramson, 1988). Private giving increased during this period, but not nearly enough to replace the cuts in government support.

In response to the increased need, nonprofit organizations have worked to enhance private giving or have sought other sources of support. For example, some members of the board of the Northwest Neighborhood Center advocate seeking greater help from local foundations or companies. Others want to raise fees for services the center provides. These three sources (government, fees, and donations) account for over 90 percent of all revenues for most human service nonprofit organizations, of which nearly half (40 percent) comes from government funding alone (Salamon, 1987). The possibility of changes in these funding levels and priorities has clearly stressed the longstanding partnership between government and nonprofit organizations, with significant implications for the tactics of nonprofit leadership.

Competing in the Marketplace

The resource problems facing Joe have rippling effects in Anytown. As with any complex system of relationships, changes in any one part of the system have consequences for other parts of the system. This was particularly the case for Joe's friend, Alice Berger, president of the Nielson Home. The home had a contract with the Northwest Neighborhood Center that would be significantly altered by the funding cut.

Alice Berger and the Nielson Home

Joe Brown's meeting with Alice Berger was a chance to explain his problems to a good friend who would need to understand the bad news about the impending cut. The Nielson Home, founded nearly seventy-five years before, provided a number of programs for emotionally troubled children and their families, including inpatient drug treatment for seriously afflicted teenagers (one of its largest programs) and training for disabled teenagers. Joe and Alice had worked closely and had become good friends in their efforts to coordinate the drug treatment programs between their two organizations. The purpose of the meeting was for Joe to share with Alice the unfavorable news about state funding for drug treatment. He quickly discovered that Alice had another set of problems as well. Joe felt bad that he would complicate her life even more, but first he wanted to hear what was on her mind.

The last three months had seen a steady decline in the inpatient population at Nielson Home. Many teenagers who were covered by insurance were apparently being placed in a new proprietary drug treatment facility that had just opened in Anytown. This facility was part of the largest for-profit health maintenance organization in the region. The facility provided excellent care, but usually for no longer than the thirty days allowed by most insurance companies. The well-run, efficient facility had found a lucrative niche in the marketplace and was good at what it was doing. Alice had provided her board with information about the growing competition in drug treatment services and suggested that this was not a short-term blip in the figures.

There was much for Joe and Alice to talk about. Alice wondered aloud whether nonprofit drug treatment centers like the Nielson Home had a future. They discussed the path taken by many former nonprofit health maintenance organizations that had converted recently to for-profit status. Vast changes were occurring in health care delivery.

They compared notes about their boards. Alice had taken pains to make sure her board included a number of leading health care professionals in addition to representatives of parents' groups and other advocates of the programs offered by the home. She had even been successful in encouraging some major business leaders to join the board. Recently, one of the newest members (the CEO of a growing company in the community) and a physician who had just left the board were discussing the various arguments for spinning off part of the home into a for-profit enterprise. In contrast to Joe, Alice had always sought board members with connections to the social, political, and economic elite of the community. With the support of such powerful community leaders the home had been able to diversify to many new service fields. However, as she explained to Joe, some powerful members were not always the best team players. Joe shared with Alice his decision to add more heavy hitters to his board. It became clearer to him that there were real trade-offs in such a strategy.

The discussion shifted to their own immediate problems. What would happen to the teenagers? Who would handle the most costly drug cases, which often required three to four months of intensive inpatient care? Alice shared her belief that the proprietary facility was creaming off insured clients, leaving nonprofits like the Nielson Home and government agencies with the indigent cases. Would the governor find more money for state contracts (at less than or equal to full cost)? How could they afford to keep the program operating and adequately staffed without full-paying clients? Would other government entities raise taxes dedicated to drug treatment? Were there any

corporations or foundations in town that could be encouraged to fund drug care? Were the public policymakers fully
aware of all these issues and the complex relationships in
the drug care system?

Another challenge of finding financial resources for nonprofit organizations comes from competitive factors in the marketplace. Alice's issue is different from Joe's and the Northwest
Neighborhood Center's and in some ways more complex. Joe's
problem is fundamentally political. For Alice the problem includes not only the politically motivated cut at the Neighborhood
Center that would affect the Nielson Home but also competition in the health care market in Anytown. Just as the nonprofit-government relation is a complex weave of patterns of
influence that Joe and his board must somehow manage, so are
the relations among nonprofit organizations, the market, and
for-profit organizations for Alice and the Nielson Home.

In a number of fields — notably health, mental health, and
recreation services — business and nonprofit enterprises are increasingly market competitors. The nature of the competitive
relations between the nonprofit and business communities is part
of a larger national debate about the place of nonprofit organizations in our economy. Although Alice Berger is understandably concerned about the survival of the Nielson Home, also
at stake is the way psychiatric (and other health care services)
are provided in our country. How can the Nielson Home compete against national chains of proprietary facilities? Should it?
At the institutional level, the relationship of the business community to the nonprofit charitable community has become increasingly contentious. Moreover, the competition between businesses and nonprofit organizations is supervised by government,
as the rule maker. Governments are thus more than simply customers of nonprofit organizations.

Nonprofit leaders who might seek to increase revenue by
offering services in the competitive marketplace are limited in
the options they can pursue. Governments define what nonprofit
organizations are and what roles they may play in the economy.
The U.S. Congress, principally through the Internal Revenue

Code, defines many of the rules and legal realities of nonprofit activities. This code establishes the regulations defining exemption from paying corporate income taxes and eligibility for tax-deductible contributions. The code specifies what purposes such organizations may pursue, what kinds of lobbying and legislative advocacy they may engage in (and how much of it), and what sources of revenues are subject to what kind of tax. These legal structures begin to explain, but only partially, how the Nielson Home and the Northwest Neighborhood Center can or cannot compete in the marketplace.

Actions by other governments add other rules and operational limitations. State governments prescribe the purposes for which nonprofit organizations may be incorporated and establish the basic requirements regarding the number of members of the board of directors, the minimum frequency of board meetings, and the use and transfer of assets. States and localities have also established, subject to constitutional free-speech guarantees clarified by the U.S. Supreme Court, charitable solicitation laws and exemptions from income, property, and sales taxes. Of course, many nonprofit organizations like the Nielson Home and Northwest Neighborhood Center have purchase-of-service contracts with agencies of state or local government to deliver specified services to specified client populations.

One option for Alice Berger and the Nielson Home is to enter the marketplace with new or different services. Federal laws and regulations concerning unrelated business income are murky and subject to continuing debate and possible change. For nonprofit organizations, unrelated business income is that derived from the sale of services or products unrelated to the accepted purposes or mission of the organization. For example, sales of advertising space in publications or of gifts and souvenirs have nothing to do with directly furthering the charitable purposes of the organization. Though the *income* from such sales often furthers the organization's charitable purposes, the *activities* (that is, the sales) are not related to those purposes. Thus, income from such activities is unrelated business income. Such income is subject to federal unrelated business income tax (UBIT). Recent changes in UBIT regulations may have substantial effects on the management of nonprofit organizations and their role in the marketplace.

In response to the circumstances facing the Nielson Home and the Northwest Neighborhood Center, it is possible that the leaders will turn to tactics to boost earned income (both mission-related and unrelated) if increases in private giving are not sufficient to make up for lost revenue. Recent decreases in marginal tax rates and changes in deductions of appreciated property may also work against further increases in contributions. Attempts to increase earned income most likely will come through increasing fees for mission-related services and creating new mission-related programs that bring in additional revenues. For example, Joe Brown can recommend to his board that they increase the fees for the drug treatment program, and Alice Berger can expand her psychiatric services to include other inpatient treatment programs (if the market will bear it). These two nonprofits may also find themselves venturing into activities designed to increase passive and unrelated income. The continuing possibility of legislation and regulations that may substantially limit or penalize such unrelated income opportunities creates significant challenges for Joe and Alice.

Working with the Charitable and Philanthropic Community

Whatever the outcomes of attempts by nonprofit organizations to increase earned income, the reliance upon private giving will continue to be significant for many nonprofits. Joe's friend Alice Berger finds herself with a dilemma created by the Nielson Home's reliance upon foundation support. Working with the charitable and philanthropic community is an important facet of the challenge to find financial resources.

Alice hung up the telephone. It was not the best way to start another day. An officer from the XYZ Foundation had called to ask if the Nielson Home had actively sponsored yesterday's demonstration at the XYZ corporate headquarters. The demonstrators, led by a staff physician from the home, had called attention to what they asserted was XYZ's discrimination against the disabled in hiring and promotion. Alice told the officer that the home had not sponsored or been involved in any way in promoting the demonstration.

When the foundation officer asked if she had known this was coming and if she had tried to stop the physician, Alice replied that she had heard about these plans but had neither encouraged nor discouraged the physician. Private individuals were free to do what they felt necessary. The foundation officer asked, "But aren't you worried that *your* staff is biting the hand that feeds them? We are embarrassed by this whole affair; it has been covered by the local media, and the position taken by the doctor and his employment at the Nielson Home are clearly identified in the newspaper."

While the grants the home had recently received from XYZ Foundation were not especially large, XYZ's prestige in the community could help open doors to other foundations and corporations. Alice wondered if she should talk to the physician. She told the foundation officer that almost all her staff were social activists of one stripe or another; otherwise, why would a physician be willing to work for so little at the Nielson Home? As these comments were greeted with silence by the foundation officer, Alice was sorry she had made them.

From the perspective of the nonprofit executive, the challenges in dealing with the philanthropic community are much more complex than simply applying for a grant and awaiting a positive response. Those who have a stake in the organization will work in ways to influence its operations and its resources. A nonprofit organization is effective to the extent that it meets the needs and demands of individuals, groups, or organizations (stakeholders) concerned with its activities. The stakeholders are both those groups without whose support the organization would cease to exist and those who would be most seriously affected if the organization were to cease providing a service (Bryson, 1988).

Working with stakeholders can affect relationships with foundations. Activities aimed at satisfying stakeholders are often of a social or political nature, and their resolution is found in the external environment of the organization. Satisfied stakeholders are often the strongest and the best advocates of an organization's interests. Strategically placed advocates who can reach the influential people in a community can influence resources providers. Obviously, the reliance upon foundations for financial resources requires a special kind of political skill. Foundation leadership is intricately connected to the social and political leadership of the community. In smaller communities, they all may be the same people. Foundations fund agencies that they believe have the greatest probability of successfully handling important problems. The proven track record of a nonprofit organization is critical. (Although some foundations take greater risks in funding less well-known applicants, most approach funding decisions conservatively.) Most important is the visibility and perceived credibility of the organization in the eyes of the funder. The track record of the chief executive is an important consideration. The inclusion of heavy hitters on a board can bring such credibility. The careful treatment of a problem like the one Alice faces with XYZ Foundation is essential.

The purpose of this first chapter has been to characterize the special challenges of executive leadership in nonprofit organizations. Two special challenges are identified: finding financial resources and clarifying responsibilities between the volunteer board and the executive director. Success in meeting these challenges is attained by understanding the unique dependence of these organizations upon resources controlled by external interests. Finding resources is complicated by the multiple sources from which funding can come. Some are found in government, some are to be found in the philanthropic community of foundations, corporations, and individual givers, and some derive from operations in the marketplace.

The challenges are exacerbated by changing priorities on the political agenda and by the need to establish good relationships with the philanthropic community. Decisions about how to deal with these issues are complicated by the often tangled relations between an executive and a volunteer board. In addition, the leaders of nonprofit organizations are expected both to run an efficient internal management system and to operate skillfully across the boundaries of the nonprofit organization. In short, the leadership of nonprofit organizations calls for a very special set of proficiencies.

TWO

Understanding Nonprofit Organizations and Their Environment

०००

The challenges facing leaders of nonprofit organizations are to a large extent the consequence of the complicated relationship between nonprofit organizations and the government, the marketplace, and the philanthropic community. Most simply put, nonprofit organizations are part of a system of interacting components in which a change in one component affects others. At the most general level it is also useful to describe the nonprofit organization as "open." An open system is one that interacts with its environment; it is more than just a set of interrelated elements.

The Open Systems Approach to Defining Nonprofit Organizations

The open systems approach is helpful to understanding the boundary-spanning nature of leadership in nonprofit organizations, an idea we introduced in Chapter One and will develop more fully in Chapter Four. When one takes an open systems approach, one begins by trying to understand the collective interaction of the various parts of the system. One important concept in the open systems approach recognizes that all systems have a boundary that differentiates them from others. A boundary can be social (as in an ethnic community), temporal (as in a funding cycle), physical (as in a building), or even psychological (as in a prejudice).

For organizations, boundaries are essentially established by who is inside the organization and who is outside, or, more precisely, by what behaviors are inside and what outside. Thus, when employees or volunteers are carrying out interviews with clients, their behavior is inside the boundary; when they finish work and drive home, their behavior is outside the organization's boundary. As chief executives, other staff, or board members talk with legislators or foundation officials, they are spanning the boundary.

Although the boundary serves to separate one system from another, some boundaries have more openness to allow for interaction with their environments; in other words, boundaries vary in the extent of their permeability. The degree of permeability in the boundary is critical in understanding how the system functions—how it grows, or how it withers and dies. Too little permeability may not allow the system to renew itself with the resources necessary for its survival. Too much permeability can deluge the system with change as it tries to adjust to external demands. When an environment is particularly turbulent and the system has highly permeable boundaries, a system can become easily overwhelmed. Nonprofit organizations can be characterized as having highly permeable boundaries and existing within political, social, and economic environments that are rapidly changing.

A major leadership responsibility in nonprofit organizations is to work outside the boundary of the nonprofit organization to position it in relationship to the environmental factors that affect it, particularly its resource base. The open systems idea is straightforward as applied to nonprofit organizational leadership: No nonprofit organization is self-contained. All must engage in transactions with elements of their environments to secure the inputs necessary for operation. Actions are then taken to combine and transform the inputs into outputs that other elements in the environment want or will accept. (This is often called the "throughput" process.) The typical classes of inputs include financial resources, staff (employees and volunteers), raw materials, supplies, ideas important to the organization's effectiveness, conditions of the marketplace, certain government policies, and some degree of legitimacy (that is, social approval or influence in the political and philanthropic arenas). Throughput processes are a wide variety of technologies or techniques for making changes in raw materials. Outputs are the services or products created, as well as various forms of influence. The simplicity of the open systems idea as it is characterized in Figure 2 makes it seem obvious and not really practical, at least initially. However, several less obvious implications of the open systems approach greatly enhance its practical relevance to nonprofit organizations.

Figure 2. The Open System of Nonprofit Organizations.

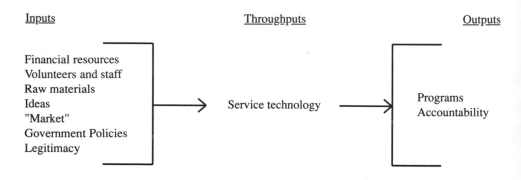

<u>Inputs</u>

<u>Throughputs</u>

<u>Outputs</u>

Financial resources
Volunteers and staff
Raw materials
Ideas
"Market"
Government Policies
Legitimacy

Service technology

Programs
Accountability

Although all organizations vary in the degree to which they are open, most nonprofit organizations have highly permeable boundaries and exceptionally complex environments compared to many businesses and government organizations. The typical nonprofit organization acquires inputs from many and varied sources. (See also Figure 1 and accompanying text in Chapter One.) Considering only financial resources, nonprofit organizations like the Nielson Home or the Northwest Neighborhood Center discussed in Chapter One may have any or all of the following: contracts with several levels and units of government, grants from several foundations and corporations, a large number of individual donors, an affiliation with a local United Way or other federated fund-raising body, a variety of earned income programs, and maybe even investment income. The nature of the transactions with each of these sources is likely to differ. In some cases the transactions are clearly commercial, with exchange of specified services for payment. In other cases the transactions are political, with exchange of favors and expectations of future support. Some transactions are of a more ambiguous nature, in which givers expect differing returns for their donations. For example, some individuals may want nothing more in return for their donations than the personal satisfaction derived from helping others. The anonymous individual giver can be contrasted with a corporate foundation that wishes full publicity about their benevolence in order to promote a positive corporate image. Many transactions may be of two or all three types. Nonprofit organizations are also highly open on many other input factors as well.

As highly open systems, nonprofit organizations have some influence, but little control, over their environments. This does not imply that nonprofit organizations are helpless. Recall Nielson Home president Alice Berger's phone call from XYZ Foundation. Alice might attempt to control the physician's participation in future demonstrations. Such an attempt is not only likely to be ineffective but is also inappropriate and unethical. Alice certainly cannot control the reaction of funders to such events. Nonetheless, Alice is not without choices. She can talk with members of the board (providing her views on the import of the foundation officer's call), invite board members' reactions, and offer her perspective that the home's values include assuring the disabled fair employment opportunities and expression of citizenship rights and obligations, noting that staff who are demonstratively committed to the mission are likely to be more effective. She can ask those board members who share this perspective to act on it by calling their friends and associates at XYZ, the XYZ Foundation, and elsewhere to communicate it and express their appreciation that XYZ and the foundation are big enough to accept this criticism and respond to it in a nonpunitive, solution-seeking way. In short, Alice and the board can promote respect for democratic rights and tolerance for disagreement. They can choose this course even if they fear some decrease in funding, while developing plans for alternative funding strategies.

The Precarious Nature of Managing in an Open System

Highly open systems are always precarious. Lots of things can go wrong (or at least change). These changes can often invite prompt action and quick fixes. Sometimes decisions have to be made straight away; opportunities are often fleeting and require prompt action. The highly open nature of nonprofit organizations requires that the organizations and their leaders be flexible and adaptive, yet principled when adapting to changes. When quick responses are necessary, decision making is facilitated when it is based upon a shared set of values and guided by the agreed-upon sense of mission for the organization.

Because nonprofit organizations are highly dependent upon external sources for financial support, the organization is not and cannot be unchanging. Missions can change with the changing needs of a community, the availability of funds, and the evolving priorities of a board. The history of a particular nonprofit program or agency may reflect a series of mergers or redefinition of mission. A rape counseling center may find itself opening a home for abused wives and children. The home itself may be operated by another nonprofit entity, such as a neighborhood housing organization. In time the home for abused wives and children may broaden its programs to include counseling for abused children and job training for abused wives. The original rape counseling service may become just one part of a more comprehensive service package.

The term *organization* suggests a thing with stable properties, including an organizational chart that prescribes authority relations, a set of jobs and roles with clear duties and responsibilities, manuals of policies and procedures covering the entire gamut of operations, and carefully developed plans. All these properties are necessary and useful, providing for continuity, predictability, and stability. They also obscure the reality that in some respects — especially in the case of highly open organizations — all organizations are constantly being re-created. As Karl Weick (1969) has suggested, perhaps we should speak of *organizing* rather than *organizations* drawing attention to the reality that organizations are never finished. It's not just that individuals receiving services come and go, it's that the interests and expectations of staff, funders, and leaders change as well. Successful leadership requires continually organizing the changing set of interests so that useful work is achieved. New strategies challenge board relationships and relations between the board and the chief executive. New funding opportunities mean new alliances and realigned priorities. Remaining open to change and being able to respond quickly and effectively is critical to the leadership of nonprofit organizations.

If nonprofit organizations are highly open to and dependent on their environments, what exactly does this mean for their leaders? We examine this question by comparing expectations for the leadership of nonprofit organizations with expectations for leadership in business and government.

Comparisons with Business

Nonprofit organizations are not businesses. If they behave only like businesses, they should not be nonprofit. However, nonprofit organizations require that the skills of effective leaders in nonprofit management be combined with skills especially relevant to business. Like business managers, nonprofit executives are expected to be proficient in managing accounting and control processes, in budgeting and financial analysis, in human resources management, in organizing efficient work processes, and in sensing the opportunities coming in the future. As one nonprofit chief executive put it in an interview: "[This organization] is not like a business. It *is* a business. If we don't make or raise enough money, we'll eventually close, no matter how important our work is." Certainly, nonprofit organizations are more likely to die than government agencies, though the nonprofit mortality rate seems to be much lower than that of small businesses. Our own view is that nonprofit organizations are, in part, businesses, and many business skills and disciplines are important for effective management.

Just as in business, the nonprofit leader is held accountable for the successes and failures of the organization. In business, with its clear measure of results, it is common to hold chief executives responsible for the profits of their organizations. Similarly, nonprofit executive leaders are generally assumed to be the principal agent of success or failure in their organizations, even though it is usually much more difficult to assess the connections between leadership action and outcomes in nonprofit organizations than in business.

The services of some nonprofit organizations are sold in competition with other nonprofits, and some nonprofits operate in direct competition with for-profit organizations. A nonprofit health facility competes directly with proprietary hospitals to attract paying or fully insured customers. Nonprofit organizations often compete directly with each other. A community-supported symphony competes with other performing arts organizations for a finite audience and a limited number of patrons for the performing arts (or competes in seeking to expand the audience). Some nonprofit organizations compete directly with each other for access to finite government or foundation dollars.

Because of this competitive governmental or foundation marketplace, nonprofit leaders often operate in businesslike ways. There are bills to pay, a bottom line to meet, and a mission to achieve. Even though nonprofit leaders do not aspire to return a profit, they often act in entrepreneurial ways in the pursuit of new funding sources (or in retaining old ones) and in establishing new programs and services. They can be expected to behave as aggressively or as defensively as the business executives to ensure the survival of their organizations. They are expected to behave this way by their boards and by those invested in their organizations because they are held accountable for the success of their organizations.

Comparisons with Government

Comparisons between public-sector executives and their counterparts in the nonprofit sector shed light upon other important expectations for nonprofit executives. In varying degrees, nonprofit organizations use public (governmental) resources to advance public (collective) interests, not just their self-interest or the interests of owners. In this respect nonprofit organizations resemble governmental organizations. Both kinds of organizations are instruments for pursuing the common good (even if there is incomplete agreement on what the common good is).

The history of the nonprofit organization in American society has been characterized by a political role that creates special expectations and responsibilities for its leaders. Mathews (1987) reminds us that, historically, the public realm of nonprofits in our democratic society is "pregovernment," even "prepolitical," as he defines it. For Mathews, civic organizations and associations (the first voluntary organizations in our history) are the taproots of our democracy, the beginnings of indirect, representative government:

> The town meetings were the beginnings of the American public, the democratic community. They provided places where "We" became "The People." It is their history that is recalled in the preamble to the Constitution.
>
> As an early political life form the town meetings evolved in two directions. They became local governments, some of which are still in existence. But as voluntary public associations, they also became the operating entities for all kinds of public works. As forums and leagues and conferences and the like, they brought their political genes to the local organization of voluntary activity throughout the country. . . . And these non-governmental organizations, I believe, continue to perform essential political functions in the little republics [Mathews, 1987, p. 4].

Mathews maintains that having a vast network of voluntary public organizations "creates an infrastructure that is essential to the strength of the social and political ecosystem of the country" (p.4). This infrastructure frames a set of values and supports an expectation that service to the public by the nonprofit voluntary sector augments the role of government, which is also conceived of as "by and for the people" and not for the benefit of a select few.

This important public side of the nonprofit organization gives rise to special expectations for its leadership. Governmental decisions are politically accountable decisions. Complex trade-offs are made by elected officials in response to the demands of a multiplicity of citizen groups. The most important decisions are debated by the press, exposing them to judgment by the interested public.

The leaders of nonprofit organizations that spend public dollars share with government executives a responsibility as guardians of the public trust. However, they are held accountable by a nonelected voluntary board as well as by government officials. Contractual arrangements are often made between governments and nonprofit organizations to deliver public services funded by public dollars. However, nonprofit executives are not *directly* overseen by elected officials and are usually subject to less scrutiny by the public and the press than are government executives. This removal of publicly supported nonprofit organizations from direct oversight by elected public officials creates real concerns about the accountability of nonprofit executives.

Thus, it should not be surprising that many nonprofit executives behave like public officials at work in the political fabric of a community. It is in the community that the public interest is defined. Today's nonprofit executive is often found bargaining, negotiating, and selling ideas like any politician. Even though many nonprofit organizations are closely aligned to the aims of government in our society, nonprofit organizations are expected to remain distinct from government. This independence is difficult to achieve to the extent that nonprofit organizations remain resource-dependent upon government. There have been many warnings that the nonprofits may be too willing to compromise their independent, private status and roles as alternatives to and critics of government by aggressively seeking government monies (for example, Nielsen, 1979).

There is much to keep in balance in maintaining autonomy while at the same time remaining accountable to elected officials. Some elected officials express concern about the implications of this balancing act. A former city mayor, for example, identifies "a political side of government" (the duly elected officials of a community); "a professional side of government" (public managers hired by the elected); and "the secret side of government" (the nonprofit sector). Nonprofit organizations deliver publicly and charitably funded services and have significant influence upon the community, he notes, but agencies, foundations, and other nonprofit entities are often free to make decisions affecting public policy without the kind of public scrutiny and citizen input he would prefer.

The conditions created by the forces of political power and philanthropic interest that shape a community and influence public policy create a complex set of problems for the effective nonprofit executive. The effective nonprofit leader plays politics in a community carefully. For example, the chief newspaper in one large city examined the role of foundations in dealing with major problems affecting the community. The executive director of a large nonprofit organization was quoted as critical of the failure of these foundations to address collectively many of the social problems in the community that had been exacerbated by insufficient government funding. The comments of the executive were reported anonymously because the executive was concerned that powerful foundation leaders might cut funding to his agency because of the criticism. The "secret side of government" identified by the mayor often remains secret because some believe dire consequences would follow if positions were taken openly. The problems of accountability and autonomy become even more complex when many nonprofit organizations ask local elected officials or politically influential individuals (or those who contribute sizable campaign funds) to join their boards.

Adhering to Multiple Community Values
and Sustaining the Mission of the Organization

The notion that nonprofit organizations are trustees, fiduciaries, or instruments of the public good is more than empty rhetoric. This idea is both the moral basis for a nonprofit organization and the impetus for its leaders to work toward its goals (within the constraints imposed by the bottom line). Though it somewhat oversimplifies reality, economists and management theorists find the idea that businesses *maximize* some single objective (whether that be profits, market share, or revenue growth) useful for both description and prescription. Both governmental units and nonprofit organizations lack such analytically useful maximization functions, although some analysts have argued that government managers attempt to maximize their units' budgets. The reality for most nonprofit organizations is that they are expected to promote many values and be accountable to many groups while furthering the organization's mission. Seldom does the mission itself provide clear guidance about what specific course of action will maximize its accomplishment. In such circumstances, good leadership requires skill in negotiation and compromise, as well as in discovering or creating courses of action that go beyond mechanical compromise.

Consider the situation facing Joe Brown of the Northwest Neighborhood Center. The state rate for support of the teenage drug treatment program will soon be cut. The program has been a means to provide teenagers with a chance to reenter their community, including programs to increase self-esteem and to prevent drug use. The center operates a number of other programs, including family counseling, after-school programs, and day care for the elderly. It is not uncommon for nonprofits like the center to have multiple contracts with different units of state and local government, to be recipients of funds from the local United Way, and to have grants from local foundations and corporations. Each of these funders expects an accurate accounting of the use of its funds, though in differing formats and with differing rules regarding use of the funds and computation of various costs. Additionally, working as it does in a multi-ethnic neighborhood, the center is expected not only to provide services equitably to differing groups but to hire, whenever possible, staff from the community and to include representatives of the various groups on the board. All these forms of accountability and multiple objectives affect mission accomplishment. What might Joe do about the funding cut in the drug treatment program in this situation, while still managing to promote the mission?

The obvious choices for Joe and the center include: abandoning the program; trying to find ways of cutting the costs of carrying out the program; and raising additional charitable funds to cover the state cut. Abandoning the program is likely to be unacceptable to many in the neighborhood and on the board. Even if cutting costs were possible, through using fewer staff for example, it might significantly lower the quality of the program and expose the center to an increased risk of dangerous incidents or even a lawsuit. Raising additional charitable funds may also be difficult. Some board members may be uncommitted to fund raising for the program, and many foundations and corporations may be unwilling to fund a program they feel the state should cover.

Are there other alternatives? One choice is to mount an effort, in conjunction with other drug treatment organizations, to restore state funding or to convince the city or county to provide additional funds to make up for the state cut. Such efforts have sometimes succeeded. A more creative possibility would be to broaden the scope of the program in relation to the mission. The drug treatment program, like many youth services, assumes that participants are both victims and potential future problems. While the program provides an opportunity for youth to return to their community drug free and with enhanced self-esteem, it treats them as clients with problems that need to be corrected. The program could additionally conceive of these teenagers (or some of them) as resources and place the young people in substantial roles designing, managing, and carrying out projects, perhaps even filling in for staff who might be lost because of the cuts (for example, in the elder day care program; see Calhoun, 1989, for a report about such programs).

This special use of teenagers as resources for the center not only advances the mission but will also be more likely to energize the board and could be attractive to corporate and foundation grant makers. Joe could discover or create this sort of alternative, but what does he do next? In asking this question, we are reminded of the open systems nature of nonprofit organizations. The teenagers can be conceived of both as recipients of the services of the organizations (outputs) and also as potential resources (inputs) for the organization. The next chapter of this book is devoted to exploring the roles of the board in this open system and the board's responsibilities in the input, thoroughput, and output processes. For the moment we want to summarize the major points of this chapter.

Nonprofit organizations are characterized as open systems, and as such the effective leadership of them is often a difficult and precarious business. Unique expectations face the leaders of nonprofit organizations as they move beyond the boundaries of their organization to operate in an environment of connections with government, with philanthropic interests, and with the marketplace. These expectations require significant skills in understanding the political and social fabric of influence in a community and often equal proficiency in attempting to influence decisions in competition with other nonprofit organizations and proprietary interests. The nonprofit organization is expected to be responsive to the government agencies from which funds are acquired while not compromising its independent status; in other words, it is expected to be competitive while remaining nonprofit.

The expectations for the effective executive combine characteristics of the successful government official and the entrepreneurial businessperson. As a businessperson, attention to the bottom line is matched by aggressive pursuit of the mission of the organization in both the business and governmental marketplaces. The fact of operating in the public sector imposes the obligation to work in the public interest while adhering to multiple community values. The effective leader is expected to be able to negotiate when values may be in conflict (that is, to be political) while maintaining a sense of mission that is independent from government (that is, to remain autonomous). Thus is the leadership of nonprofit organizations confronted with complex and often conflicting expectations.

THREE

Making Sense
of Board–Executive
Relationships

○○

In the first chapter we presented an overview of the challenges facing the U.S. nonprofit sector. We illustrated how the continuing unique characteristics as well as the changing environment of nonprofit organizations have affected leadership in such organizations. In the second chapter we undertook a more detailed examination of the nature of nonprofit organizations and how their open boundaries and dependent character affect leadership. In this chapter we complete our diagnosis of the leadership challenges by exploring the leadership roles and responsibilities of chief executives and boards. In doing so we contrast the traditional view of effective nonprofit organizational leadership with an emerging, more realistic view. This developing perspective, based on our own research and that of others, calls for abandoning, or at least substantially modifying, certain pervasive assumptions. Thus, in this chapter we first present the traditional model of nonprofit organization leadership, highlighting its prescriptive standards for board and executive roles and relationships. Next, we present the emerging alternative model and its implications for board and executive roles and relationships. We conclude by discussing how the emerging alternative provides chief executives with a more practical basis for working effectively with their boards.

37

The Traditional View of Nonprofit Organizations

Traditionally, nonprofit organizations are viewed as necessarily hierarchical in structure, with a board of directors in the superior position. From this point of view, the chief executive is hired to assist the board in its efforts to achieve the mission of the organization and works at the board's pleasure. The board is expected to oversee programs and establish standards that ensure accomplishment of the organization's mission. The board is ultimately responsible for the organization's achievements and failures.

Following Elmore (1978) we use the term "managed systems" theory to characterize this traditional hierarchical model. There are five chief propositions of managed systems theory:

1. Organizations have goals or purposes.
2. Though organizations have parts, they should operate as unitary, rational actors.
3. The mechanism to achieve rational unity of action is hierarchical control.
4. Those at the top of the hierarchy are responsible for managing the operations of the organization so that achievement of goals is maximized.
5. Effective management involves gathering information on those events and forces likely to affect goal achievement, arranging tasks to achieve the optimal level of goal attainment, and continually monitoring performance so as to adjust task arrangements.

The phrase "managed system" captures the key elements of this theory — that organizations are systems in which actions in one part are rationally connected to actions in another so as to achieve a system goal, and that the system is created and directed by leaders who make decisions and implement strategies that will result in goal achievement. Much, but certainly not all, contemporary management thinking and action is premised on this seemingly commonsense approach to describing organizations, including nonprofits.

What Is Wrong with the Traditional Model?

Just as common sense tells us incorrectly that the Earth is flat, so too the commonsense approach to explaining nonprofit organizations provides a distorted or partial understanding of organizational realities. The last three decades have seen the development of several alternative organization theories. Pfeffer, in *Organizations and Organization Theory* (1982), provides an excellent overview of both the managed systems approach (which he terms purposive-rational) and various alternatives. Here we note some of the most telling criticisms of the traditional managed systems approach and particularly observe the difficulties managed systems theory encounters in nonprofit organizations.

The notion that organizations have goals has long been criticized as crediting to an abstraction what can only be true of real individuals. How can an organization, which has no mind, be meaningfully said to have goals? Perhaps the phrase "organizational goal" is best understood as a shorthand for the summation of many individuals' goals. In the case of businesses, the individuals most likely to affect goals are the owners or top managers. Governmental and nonprofit organizations, lacking specific owners, pursue goals that some individuals have agreed upon. The fundamental point is that an organizational goal is something that specific individuals, responding to various pressures and constraints, have decided on. A goal is not something a faceless, nameless organization creates.

In nonprofit organizations the establishment of goals is likely to be especially complex. Certainly the board is expected to define and periodically review and revise the organization's mission. Little systematic empirical evidence is available to assess the respective contributions of board and staff in mission definition. One study (Herman and Tulipana, 1985) of the influence patterns in nonprofit organizations asked board members, chief executives, and senior staff from seven local health and welfare agencies to rate the influence of each group in decision making about various issues. Though mission definition was not included among the kinds of decisions studied, the results showed that board members were reported by all parties as the most influential in major financial decisions and as equal to chief executives in budget-setting decisions. In all other decision areas, such as program planning, personnel, policy and planning, and daily operations, the chief executive was regarded as the most influential. These results suggest that boards may be significantly involved in setting fundamental goals, with the chief executive playing the decisive role in defining more specific goals and objectives. An implication of this particular study is that the goal-setting process in nonprofit organizations is best understood as a complex effort on the part of *both* chief executives and board members.

In Chapter One we attempted to create a sense of the complexity found in the challenges facing Joe Brown and Alice Berger as they struggled to adapt the missions of their organizations to the rapidly changing nature of the environment in which they operate. We saw that a choice is often made to develop a program where opportunities exist rather than because a carefully conceived plan of action is implemented. Clearly, Joe and Alice's situations are inadequately described by a theory that envisions a clear, unambiguous system of control or a goal-setting process flowing from the board of directors to the chief executive and staff. The environment of nonprofit organizations is too complex to be explained in such simple theoretical terms.

Another aspect of managed systems theory that has long proved troublesome is the suggestion that although organizations have parts, they operate as unitary, rational actors. As many organizational analysts have observed, the fact that organizations have specialized departments inevitably leads to some degree of differentiation (Lawrence and Lorsch, 1967), such that managers in different units develop differing interaction styles, reporting procedures, reward criteria, and sub-goals. Such differences are useful in achieving unit objectives but often hinder overall coordination and unity of action. For example, in business the differentiation between production and sales has frequently been a source of conflict. In many nonprofit organizations the differing perspectives between service delivery and fund-raising units, between paid professionals and volunteers, and between clinically prepared and management-trained staff also make achieving unity difficult. Lawrence and Lorsch (1967) explain how successful organizations develop integrative structures and relationships in order to provide better coordination across the differentiated parts of the organization. We believe that successful nonprofit organizations have also developed such integrative structures, which require patterns of relationship that are more lateral than the vertical relationships presumed by traditional theory.

In response to the inadequacy of the unitary-actor idea, conceptions of organizations as politicized arenas in which power struggles are common have gained credence and popularity (Morgan, 1986; Pfeffer, 1982). While such a perspective has many implications for individual behavior (for example, how to succeed at organizational politics), it does not suggest how to reduce conflict to achieve more unity of action. Yet many management practices — such as profit-sharing schemes, *ad hoc* project groups, matrix structures, and win-win negotiating strategies within the organization (Fisher and Ury, 1983) — can best be understood as attempts to effectively use differing interests. Astute nonprofit executives must always be aware that differentiation creates the possibility of power struggles and that achieving something approaching unity of action requires continual conflict resolution and integrative efforts.

Hierarchy is an aspect of every organization. As Perrow (1986) has observed, hierarchy seldom gets the credit it deserves. When effective decisions are made and work is going well, cooperation and coordination are credited. When things go wrong hierarchy, or bureaucratic red tape more generally, are blamed. Nevertheless, hierarchy sometimes creates as many problems as it solves. Many scholars and practitioners have noted that hierarchy provides for positional or formal authority but does not ensure that information and expertise are correspondingly aligned. Indeed, in organizations dependent on professionally trained specialists, the separation between positional authority and competence and information is frequently substantial. This disjunction often requires alternatives to strictly hierarchical approaches to decision making and problem solving.

Because many nonprofit organizations are heavily professionalized and/or relatively small, hierarchy is often deemphasized, though hardly nonexistent.

We believe the most potentially complex aspect of hierarchical control in many nonprofit organizations is the relationship between the board and the chief executive. As we have noted already, the board is usually placed on the organization chart at the top. (Some charts put the community at the very top—a symbolic practice that may help to remind board and staff of the importance of their role as public trustees but seems unlikely to affect actual practice in most cases.) Ordinarily, the chief executive is placed below the board. Currently, some nonprofit organizations are adopting a corporate model in which the chief executive's title is "president" rather than "executive director" and he or she is a voting member of the board. Even in this case, the chief executive is assumed to remain subordinate to the board. Both legal standards and virtually all the substantial prescriptive literature on nonprofit boards place the board at the top of the hierarchy. For example, as Houle (1989, p. 7) has written: "Since a board has ultimate authority in fulfilling the mission of its agency, it must have ultimate control over it."

Prescriptive Standards of the Managed Systems Model for Nonprofit Organizations

The previous section described the general tenets of the traditional, managed systems approach and its shortcomings when applied to nonprofit organizations. Here we examine the more specific prescriptive principles of the model, particularly board and executive roles and relationships. The prescriptive standards are founded on both a legal requirement and a moral assumption. The law requires that a nonprofit board be held ultimately responsible for the affairs and conduct of the organization. The moral assumption is that a board will conduct the affairs of the organization as a public steward. The board, in other words, should see that the organization serves the interests of the larger community. Thus, nonprofit boards are legally and morally responsible for the conduct of the organization. Certain additional prescriptions follow from these foundations.

Given the legal and moral requireme
cepts its responsibilities and carries out its
and decision-making roles. While the exe(
tion of the board, provides information and
makes major policy decisions — about en_
programs, about financing, and about managing ιτς ᴄ
The chief executive's role is to implement the policies determineᴅ
by the board. This standard invokes the familiar distinction between policy and administration. Public administration scholars and practitioners have long struggled with this dichotomy.
Late in the nineteenth century Woodrow Wilson argued that
the making of public policy (that is, politics) must be solely the
province of elected officials; the task of civil servants was strictly
administering policies. Wilson argued that if unelected (and thus,
unaccountable) civil servants made policy, then the basis of democracy was undermined. By and large, however, students of
public administration have concluded that no rigid distinction
between policy and administration is possible. Nonetheless, the
distinction remains a popular idea. Such is certainly the ᴄasᴄ
in the nonprofit sector as well. In our own work with nonprofit
organizations we have often encountered the desire for this distinction to be affirmed.

The policy-administration distinction corresponds to reality enough to be appealing. It is possible to conceptually or ver-
bally separate these activities. Though few promote the idea that
the two can always be clearly separated in practice, some writers
on nonprofit boards continue to argue the usefulness of the distinction. For instance, Chait and Taylor (1989) suggest that nonprofit boards will be more effective if they understand that their
role differs with differing policy levels. They distinguish six
levels — major, secondary, functional, minor, standard operating procedures, and rules. A board's role also varies with the
stages of policy development, which are characterized as defining policy objectives, formulation, implementation, and evaluation. Chait and Taylor conclude that a board's attention "should
be concentrated on developing higher level policy objectives and
statements and then, on a selective basis, on executing and monitoring important policies" (p. 53). These authors do not specify
the executive's and the staff's role, but the tone of their remarks

plies an expectation that the executive and senior staff will also be involved in all levels and stages of policy. Thus, Chait and Taylor reaffirm at least half the policy-administration principle: The board's role is that of setting and evaluating major policies.

Another writer and consultant on nonprofit boards advocates a framework for governance that resembles the policy-administration prescription. Carver (1980) uses the ends-means distinction and sees the board's role as specifying ends (what it is that the organization is to achieve). That is, the board is responsible for determining policy, but policy statements need to be put in the form of ends or outcomes to be achieved, rather than means or process to be used. It then becomes the executive's and the staff's role to select means to achieve the board-specified ends. However, Carver maintains that the board must also set certain limits to the executive's discretion in choosing means. The board is also charged with monitoring or evaluating the extent to which ends have been achieved and proscribed means avoided. Carver's framework thus more thoroughly recapitulates the policy-administration formula, but with the helpful improvement of clearly identifying policy as an issue of ends and administration as a matter of means.

Both approaches are appropriate and useful in a general way. Boards should concentrate on the fundamental ends of the enterprise. The trouble comes in applying the generally accepted principle in specific circumstances. The problems, opportunities, and changing conditions that any nonprofit organization faces do not come labeled as "major policy" or "administrative means." Not only must a board and an executive sort out what are their major policies and ends, they must also be prepared to adjust them as conditions change. The rapidity and ambiguity of change make simple policy-administration and ends-means standards impossible to consistently implement.

Indeed, the standards of the traditional model — that the board must accept its legal and moral responsibilities, define the ends and major policies of the organization, carefully delegate administrative implementation to staff, and evaluate and redefine ends — are widely recognized as demanding and difficult to achieve. To help make these standards more achievable, a number of more specific prescriptions have been widely advocated. These prescriptions constitute what has been called the "heroic" ideal of board leadership (Herman, 1989) and include the following:

1. The board uses a systematic process to assess the strengths and weaknesses of the board's composition, usually through a board profile of demographic characteristics and experiences and skills.
2. The board profile identifies the characteristics and skills desired in new members.
3. Recruitment of potential members is systematic and rigorous. Candidate members are thoroughly informed about the organization's mission, goals, and financial condition and the time, effort, and level of contributions expected from them. Candidates are interviewed by a board committee and perhaps the entire board as to their motives and interest in voluntary board service.
4. New members receive additional orientation and training, not only from the chief executive but from other board members.
5. Directors commit significant time and effort to their duties, not only attending committee and board meetings, but also preparing for meetings and undertaking other activities.
6. Meetings are characterized by a process through which all are encouraged to participate and disagreement is welcomed, while relationships are collegial and decision making consensual. The board works as a team.
7. The board assesses the performance of the board as a whole as well as of individual members. The board uses guidelines to remove those who fail to meet minimum expectations.
8. The board's chief tasks are to define and periodically reevaluate the organization's mission and programs, to develop a strategic plan, to approve budgets and policy statements consistent with the plan, to ensure that the resources necessary to achieve the plan are obtained, and to establish and

carry out appropriate financial control and oversight procedures, including an annual independent audit.

9. The board must select, evaluate, and, if necessary, dismiss the chief executive.

A Case Study of the Inadequacy of the Traditional Model's Standards of Board Leadership

In the traditional model, the selection of the chief executive is an occasion when the decision-making authority of the board can be assumed to be total and the board's influence over the direction of the organization the most compelling. The authority of the board to appoint is also the authority to dismiss. Of all the decisions that give the board power over the organization, surely it is control over the chief executive's hiring and firing that constitutes its final authority. The selection (or dismissal) of the chief executive is one of the most tangible and important functions of the board. This decision can serve as an occasion to examine goals and to redirect programs and mission.

However, determining who should run the organization may not always be as straightforward as hiring or firing the chief executive. Often boards (particularly of smaller organizations) assign specific administrative responsibility to individual board members, depending on the capabilities of the chief executive. For example, a board member with accounting experience may have responsibility to oversee the financial control process, or even to perform the bookkeeping operations. In these instances, the choice of a board member to perform a specific administrative role must be made with great care. Handling oversight and determining accountability becomes a delicate matter. Firing a board member who inadequately performs an assigned administrative function can be sticky business.

In short, the assignment of responsibility and the determination of accountability in a nonprofit organization is a complex endeavor. However, from the traditional perspective, the board's authority is final. In the case of executive selection, the board has absolute authority to find and hire the right executive. A good example of this point of view is developed by Houle

(1989, pp. 105–108), who outlines the following basic steps a board should follow in the selection process:

1. Decide whether the process will be handled solely by the board or whether an outside consultant will be hired.
2. Decide upon the special criteria to be established for the new executive.
3. Decide on the extent to which staff or others should advise the board in the decision.
4. Create a special search committee to build a list of candidates.
5. Choose from the list of candidates those best suited for the position.
6. Make an offer to the best candidate and be precise and clear about all terms of employment.
7. Induct the new director into the special aspects of the job.

These seven steps are important ones in the selection process, and Houle provides helpful advice about how to proceed through them. But many selection decisions do not occur in such straightforward ways. Many factors can influence the decision taken; the authority and responsibility may be clearly the board's, but the patterns of influence that shape the decision can be complex.

To cite just one example, Zald (1965) describes the parrying of power between a divided board and a retiring chief executive who played a strategic role in the choice between two candidates as his successor. This succession struggle occurred in a large service organization. The principal actors were Mr. Heis, the chief executive, who originally wished his successor to be chosen six months before his retirement, and two final candidates. One, Mr. Leaf, was a younger and more innovative aspirant who was preferred by Heis. The other finalist, Mr. Maddy, was older and represented a more traditional element of the organization. He was preferred by a powerful segment on the board.

The organization had traditionally provided a wide range of preventative and socialization programs for relatively well-adjusted members of its community. It had not emphasized programs of rehabilitation and resocialization of maladjusted individuals. Zald observes that the organization's goals focused on "character development" rather than "rehabilitation or reclamation" (p. 54).

Zald suggests that three organizational characteristics of this agency are important in understanding the succession process. First, its goals (like those of many nonprofit organizations) were rather broadly stated, for example, "to develop the character" of its clients. Second, its emphasis was on preventative programs. The organization typically served the well-adjusted in order to prevent them from developing "deviant characteristics and help them to develop positive ones" (p. 54). Third, lay (board) control of the programs was strongly emphasized by the staff, with great pains taken to ensure the board's active role in deciding the work of the agency.

"These three organization features condition the succession process in important ways," notes Zald. "First, the search for a successor can involve more than just a search for an effective administrative leader, someone who can implement established goals. Because goals are broadly defined, the question of who succeeds to positions of authority may involve the organization's mission. Almost all organizations have 'traditionalists' and 'progressives,' those who are satisfied with the status quo and those who work for change and realignment. However, in welfare or service organizations with broadly defined missions, in contrast to business organizations, the discussion among traditionalists and progressives affects more than just the choice of means — it affects basic definitions of goals as well" (p. 55).

Both Leaf and Maddy were internal candidates for the job. Leaf, the candidate of choice of the retiring executive, had been interviewed for a similar job in another city. Since Heis favored Leaf, he asked the board to put forward the decision before Leaf took the other job. The president of the board of directors, in consultation with Heis, agreed to have an enlarged executive committee of the board consider the issue, and the president recommended this action to the full board. Although Leaf had the backing of Heis, his advocates on the board were hardly in control. Maddy appeared a stronger favorite, being older and representing the more traditional view of the organization. Maddy had a long association with many of the more substantial board members — powerful bankers, investment brokers, and other conservative members. Maddy represented "the preventative and middle-class orientation of the organization," and Leaf "strongly identified with social welfare and liberal [progressive] points of view" (p. 50).

A "full discussion of the directions the board wanted to take" was called for and "a full analysis of the candidates" was to guide the decision (p. 50). All final candidates (five external candidates were added to the list) were to be asked by the executive committee for their views on three key questions, one dealing with the future of the organization, another dealing with its competition from other agencies, and the third dealing with its capacity for expanding its services. Zald provides us with another key bit of information: Heis believed that preventative programs would not be as relevant as before. He believed that conditions in the community served by the agency were changing and that the organization needed to alter its mission to include rehabilitative services.

This selection process favored Leaf in certain ways. First, including several external candidates altered the unspoken expectation that Maddy was the natural successor. Second, the selection process gave Leaf exposure to a group of board members with whom he had had little interaction. Third, in the discussion of programs and mission, Leaf would be seen as more articulate and forward-looking.

During the course of the board's discussion, Leaf began to appear as a serious contender. However, at a critical point in the discussion, one of the more traditional board members accused Leaf of being ill-suited as an administrator. Heis was asked to comment, and he "presented to the executive committee evidence from annual ratings of executive personnel which disproved the charges" (p. 57). At this point in the deliberations, Heis was asked directly by an important board member for his opinion, and Heis explicitly endorsed Leaf. Leaf was chosen executive director. According to Zald, "Throughout the discussion, the [chairman of the board] did not take an assertive role, essentially serving as a discussion leader rather than as a prime mover. But he did use his power as chairman of the executive committee at the last meeting preceding the announcement of the executive committee's nomination to the full Board. At this time the Board member who had questioned Leaf's administrative abilities tried to reopen the question. The [chairman] strongly asserted his role and argued that the process had been a fair one and that all relevant considerations had been discussed, thus cutting off further debate" (p. 57).

On the surface, it was the board that chose Leaf as successor to Heis. However, below the surface cross-currents of influence were exercised by the retiring director that had significant impact upon the final choice. If Leaf had not received initial support, instigated by Heis, the board would have chosen Maddy no matter what Heis desired. It is relatively certain that had Heis remained neutral, or had he been less skillful in how he exercised influence (for example, had he lost his standing with the board president or been viewed as manipulative by the board), Maddy would have been selected. Would the agency ultimately have redefined its mission to engage in rehabilitative care under Maddy's leadership? In light of Maddy's orientation and the power of the conservative members of the board, one can only speculate that changes in the mission would have been slow in coming.

Heis's actions are characteristic of how many effective nonprofit executives work. Were the best interests of the community served? Can standards of effectiveness be determined against which to address this issue in light of Heis's actions? These are not simple questions, and the answers are complex.

As a consequence of the selection of Leaf, the organization redefined its mission and became more involved with rehabilitation, which was a growing need in the community. To suggest that the selection of Leaf was the board's alone or that the redefinition in mission was a rational decision made by the board as representatives of community needs is to mask the strategic effect of Heis's actions. One might certainly make the case that the interests of the community were well served by the selection of Leaf at Heis's instigation. It is a judgment call.

In any case, we are not trying to decide here whether the actions taken by Heis were right or wrong. The key issue we are addressing is the inadequacy of the traditional model to describe effective leadership in nonprofit organizations. We believe that advocating an apolitical decision process is inconsistent with the realities of the way key decisions get made in nonprofit organizations. Following the rational and purposive steps in the selection process advocated by Houle is only a beginning. To assume that executives like Heis do not nor should not become involved in the selection process is unrealistic. On the surface the seven steps advanced by Houle were systematically followed. Below the surface a much different selection process was carried out.

The alternative model we will propose allows a much more valid description of what happened. In spite of the widespread belief in the validity of the prescriptive hierarchical model, many experienced practitioners have noted that reality does not usually match the model.

For example, Brian O'Connell, president of Independent Sector, has observed (1985, p. 52): "The greatest source of friction and breakdown in voluntary organizations of all types, sizes, ages and relative degrees of sophistication and excellence relates to misunderstandings and differing perceptions between the voluntary [board] president and staff directors." The continuing role ambiguity and conflict between chief executives and boards has a number of sources. In recalling the experiences of Joe Brown in Chapter One, we are reminded of the difference between the formal authority of his board and the information he holds about both the funding crisis and the operational problems of the Northwest Neighborhood Center. It is Joe who must argue the case for the center in the state capital, and it is Joe who must negotiate or renegotiate contracts with other agencies if the center's funds are cut. As we have noted, chief executives like Joe nearly always hold much more organizationally relevant information than the board, as well as greater expertise in a variety of organizationally relevant fields. Joe Brown's career and professional identity are invested in his knowledge base and the viability of the center's programs. Further, the work of the organization is generally a central life interest for him as it is not for board members. It pays his bills. These realities and others lead, we believe, to divergence between the prescriptive ideal of the managed systems perspective and the actual practices of nonprofit organizations.

The prescriptive focus of the traditional model of nonprofit organizations has put the board of directors at the *top* of the hierarchy and at the *center* of organizational leadership. Both researchers and practitioners have recognized that boards usually fall far short of achieving the heroic role ascribed to them (see Middleton's useful summary, 1987; as well as Middleton, 1989; Fink, 1989; and Heimovics and Herman, 1990, for detailed analyses). The traditional model, nonetheless, continues to be widely propounded as desirable and obtainable. Why should this be so, if indeed the traditional model is almost always inaccurate and unrealistic? We believe there are three reasons for the continued preeminence of the traditional view.

First, as observed earlier, the traditional model is consistent with the legal responsibility assumed by nonprofit boards of directors. Though the legal standards for directors of public charities fall ambiguously somewhere between the law of trusts and the law of business corporations (Middleton, 1987), it is clear that directors can be held liable for failing to oversee the financial management of nonprofit organizations. Thus, the law places directors in a position of ultimate responsibility, even if the precise meaning of that responsibility remains unclear.

Second, the traditional model provides desirable and valued standards. The fundamental justification for nonprofit organizations is that they are vehicles through which individuals jointly and *voluntarily* undertake to provide public services that are not adequately or appropriately provided by business or government. As voluntary organizations, they more fully justify their legal privileges and public support to the extent that they are directed by citizen volunteers. The heroic board model thus serves both as a standard for gauging performance and as a target at which to aim. Challenging standards can be useful in generating higher levels of performance. However, standards that are virtually unobtainable soon lose all motivating force.

Third, the traditional model has remained preeminent due

to the lack of an alternative. Despite the recognized gap between prescription and reality, no compelling alternative model has been proposed. It's not especially difficult to describe the shortcomings of the traditional model and its heroic standards. It is difficult to develop an alternative model that is both grounded in empirical reality and that provides useful standards, where those standards are consistent with legal responsibilities and the values of the nonprofit sector.

The Emerging Alternative Model

Our own work, as well as that of other researchers, convinces us that an alternative model *is* emerging. For example, Young (1987) treats the executive, rather than the board, of the nonprofit organization as the organization's entrepreneur. Young argues that a primary concern of the executive is the constantly changing nature of the environment of the organization, which "either threatens (the organization's) source of sustenance or creates new opportunities for development" (p. 160). Young also notes the increasing dependence of nonprofit organizations on government programs and policies. He argues that the executive must actively seek to define and redefine the direction of an agency by adapting to changes created by this dependency. In a similar vein, Smith (1989) maintains that entrepreneurship by the chief executive is the key to the effectiveness of the nonprofit organization's growth and survival. He describes *entrepreneurism* as "taking advantage of growth opportunities, being conscious of costs and expenditures, and taking the organization into new and different service areas" (p. 598). Drucker (1990) is quite clear about the centrality of the role of the chief executive in the leadership of nonprofit organizations. "What works is to assign responsibility for the effective governance of the organization to the executive officer" (p. 13). For Drucker it is the chief executive in the well-functioning nonprofit organization who must assure that the governance function is properly organized and maintained.

Gronbjerg's (1989) research also complements this perspective. She has carefully studied patterns and changes in the patterns of funding of nonprofit social service agencies and the impact of these shifting streams of resources on organizational structure and work. Gronbjerg concludes that the overall growth or stability of the agencies studied conform closely to the agencies' experience with changing public funds. Gronbjerg argues that management actions—for example, the kind that most likely would be initiated by the chief executive, the maintenance by the chief executive of existing funding relationships, and the leverage these relationships provide in securing continuing funding—have the strongest influence on how well resource dependency is handled. A conclusion that might be drawn from her careful study is that the complexity, timing, and amount of work involved in managing the volatility of funding is in many ways beyond the scope of the board's work.

Pfeffer (1981) suggests that organizational power goes to those who have control or can influence some critical organizational resource. For nonprofit organizations, this hypothesis implies that the conditions created by wide-ranging shifts in the patterns of funding place significant organizational power in the hands of the executive. In Pfeffer's formulation, the emphasis is on the social power that is derived from the ability to influence the kinds of resources on which the organization most depends. If the chief executive's actions are deemed central to the resolution of the problems created by these factors, Pfeffer's argument would suggest that a special kind of power accrues to the chief executive—a power distinct from that which might accrue to a board less centrally involved in resolving problems of resource dependency.

The alternative model evolving from the arguments of these researchers we believe is more realistic and consequently more practical than the traditional model. It describes how things actually work in effective nonprofit organizations. Nonetheless, the alternative is consistent with nonprofit boards' legal responsibilities and the public sector's values. It does not abandon the critically important role of the board. The model is built on the reality that, in most cases, the *chief executive is the center of leadership for the organization*. And for us the most important leadership functions are those actions that are necessary to secure the resources required to achieve the organization's mission.

There are clearly instances in which the chief executive is not the center of leadership. Organizations composed solely of volunteers obviously find leadership from volunteers. Similarly, in many start-up nonprofit organizations, even after they've hired some staff, volunteer founders continue to be the central leadership figures. In spite of these and other possible exceptions to the general reality, we believe that in most established, staffed nonprofit organizations chief executives come to be expected by board members, other staff, and themselves to be finally responsible for the successes and failures of the organization.

Evidence for this crucial finding comes principally from our study of how nonprofit chief executives, board presidents, and staff assign responsibility for success or failure in critical organizational events (see Heimovics and Herman, 1990, for technical details). The research methods we used are especially useful at getting beneath the expressed models of organizational leadership that people like to think they use to the actual workings of leadership in particular instances. We asked those chief executives who voluntarily agreed to participate in our research to first recall and describe a recent critical event that turned out successfully. We then asked them to similarly recall and describe another recent critical event that turned out unsuccessfully. Finally, the executives assessed, using standard attributional rating techniques, the extent to which each of several factors contributed to the outcome of each critical event.

Summaries of the events were sent to board presidents and certain senior staff involved in each event. They were asked to rate the extent to which each event was important and the extent to which each turned out successfully or unsuccessfully. They substantially agreed with the chief executives' ratings of importance and successfulness. The board presidents and senior staff were also asked to assess the extent to which each of the same several factors contributed to the outcome of each event.

It's in these assessments (or attributions) of what caused the outcomes that the reality of the central leadership responsibility of chief executives is revealed. In critical events that turned out successfully, executives, board presidents, and staff all credited executives with contributing most to that outcome. Surprisingly, in critical events that turned out unsuccessfully, all again saw the chief executive as the most responsible for that outcome. In these unsuccessful events, board presidents and staff assigned more responsibility for the outcome to others (especially the chief executive) and to bad luck than to themselves. Chief executives, in contrast, took responsibility for the unsuccessful outcomes, assigning more responsibility to themselves than to others or to bad luck. Interestingly, despite the central role ascribed to boards, board presidents assigned relatively little responsibility to themselves in either successful or unsuccessful events. In short, whether things go well or badly, all fingers, including his or her own, point to the chief executive as centrally responsible.

What does the reality of the central leadership role of chief executives imply for rethinking the roles and responsibilities of boards and executives? Two very different scenarios are possible. On the one hand, since chief executives are going to be held responsible, perhaps they should assume full control, running things as they think best. The board then becomes either the proverbial rubber stamp or a combination rubber stamp and cash cow. Certainly these patterns are not unknown already. On the other hand, since chief executives are going to be held responsible, and since they do accept responsibility for mission accomplishment and public stewardship, perhaps they should work to see that boards fulfill their legal, organizational, and community roles. We advocate this second option, not only because it is consistent with legal requirements and voluntaristic values, but also because, as our other research findings demonstrate, it is more likely to lead to organizational effectiveness.

Effective Leadership in Nonprofit Organizations

The assertion that organizational effectiveness is enhanced by chief executives taking responsibility, if necessary, for board development and performance is neither unsupported deduction nor wishful thinking. Empirical evidence supports this argument. A major goal of our recent research program was to determine what behaviors or skills distinguished especially effective nonprofit chief executives from others not rated as especially effective. This research (see Herman and Heimovics, 1987 and 1990, for technical details) investigated whether a sample of nonprofit chief executives rated highly effective by knowledgeable observers (that is, foundation and United Way officials and heads of technical assistance and coalition organizations) differed in leadership behaviors from a comparison sample of chief executives not regarded as especially effective. Given the crucial importance of chief executives in nonprofit organizations, we were interested in the extent to which each of the two groups in our sample (effective and comparison) engaged in specific leadership behaviors both in relation to staff and in relation to the board.

We found first that staff and board leadership require independent and distinct sets of behavioral skills. It is thus necessary to differentiate between leadership behaviors directed at the board and those directed at the staff. Second, we discovered that the especially effective executives and the comparison group did not differ in the extent of leadership provided to staff (both executive samples provided substantial leadership to staff). However, effective executives provided substantially more leadership for their boards than those in the comparison group; that is, they took responsibility for providing board-centered leadership. We consider this a most significant finding to support our alternative model of leadership in nonprofit organizations.

More specifically, we found that effective executives work with their boards to facilitate interaction both within the board and between themselves and the board. They attend to board members' feelings and needs, envision changes in organizational functioning, promote and reinforce board accomplishments, and provide useful decision-making information to the board. In Chapter Four we discuss the implications of these findings for the leadership functions of resource acquisition and maintenance engaged in by the chief executive. In Chapter Five we present detailed information on practicing these characteristics of board-centered leadership. In the balance of this chapter we discuss the implications of our alternative model for the role of the board.

Prescriptive Standards of the Alternative Model of Nonprofit Organizations

The prescriptive (or practical) implications of the emerging alternative model start with the same legal reality as the traditional managed systems model: The nonprofit board is ultimately legally responsible. The moral assumption—that a board will conduct the affairs of the organization as a public steward—is also retained as an ideal, but there is no assumption that this will usually happen. Rather, we assert that such public stewardship is much more likely to occur if, and only if, the chief executive helps the board to understand and carry out this responsibility, as well as its legal responsibility. Thus, the legal and moral responsibilities of the board remain foundational. However, the alternative model recognizes that boards are most likely to meet these responsibilities only if the board and chief executive share leadership.

The alternative model differs from the traditional in other important ways. Whereas the traditional model places decision making about major policies substantially (if not solely) in the board's purview, the alternative model embraces the necessity that decision making is a responsibility shared by the board and chief executive, as well as other staff. As Brian O'Connell (1985, p. 44) has observed: "The worst illusion ever perpetrated in the nonprofit field is that the board of directors makes policy and the staff carries it out. This is just not so." Attempts to separate policy from administration are seen as both practically impossible and unproductive. Such distinctions are, in practice, impossible, because policy is meaningless except as it is actually implemented. Distinctions of what is policy and what is administrative implementation will change as circumstances change. Spending time and effort on classifying possible future events as policy or administration may often be less productive than getting on with the job.

This is not to imply that the board is involved in everything. The alternative model accepts that chief executives will be important participants in the decision process; given their own and staff expertise, and given the extensive array of organizationally relevant information available to them, chief executives are always fundamentally involved in organizational decisions. Rather than pretend otherwise, the alternative accepts this and conceives of the executive's role as encouraging consensual decision making on the important issues as they arise.

In the alternative model, the standards of the heroic ideal of boards continue to be recognized as desirable. They provide the bases for developing effective consensual decision making. However, in the alternative model, the chief executive becomes responsible for providing leadership in achieving these standards. The fundamental difference between the prescriptive standards of the traditional managed systems model and those of the alternative model is that the latter no longer puts the board at the center of leadership in nonprofit organizations. Boards are still expected to do much, but they are not expected to do things on their own. Chief executives are expected to provide board-centered leadership. Chief executives do not usurp the board's roles and responsibilities, however. Rather, effective chief executives know that helping their boards to meet their responsibilities is the best way to maximize their effectiveness.

Reviewing Management Decisions and Chief Executive Performance Appraisal in the Alternative Model

The traditional model holds that the board must review all significant management decisions and assess the performance of the chief executive against the achievement of the organization's mission, as well as against more precise objectives. However, as we have noted, the board is fundamentally dependent upon the chief executive for information and expertise. The executive holds much more organizationally relevant information and has substantial control and discretion over its presentation. We know that boards do not just make policies and have chief executives carry them out and then assess how effectively the executive has implemented policy. Successful chief executives play an active policy role as they deal with such matters as clarifying the organization's mission, stabilizing sources of funding, engaging in politics in the community, and becoming involved in other goal-setting, strategic planning, and policy-setting matters.

In light of the difficulty in separating the work of the board from the work of the executive, how can a board oversee its chief executive when it is so fundamentally reliant upon that chief executive for information? Our conclusion is that in most cases (except for clear-cut instances of unethical conduct or gross administrative failure) it is impossible for a board to evaluate the chief executive in terms of quantitative goal achievement. While annual plans that include specific outcome goals are necessary and useful, many unpredictable events can occur to make some specific outcomes unattainable. Thus, an annual plan might specify a 10 percent increase in donations, no increase in unit costs, or successful completion of an accreditation review. However, a local economic downturn, a rapid rise in the inflation rate, or delays by an accrediting body may put achieving these goals beyond the executive's ability. In our view annual plans with specific targets are important, but they cannot be applied mechanically in an executive's performance evaluation. Nor are such specific goals the only or most important criteria for executive evaluation.

Rather, it is our belief that boards can and should hold their executives accountable for the quality of leadership actions they take vis-a-vis the board and for the extent to which an executive works to ensure that the eight standards we have identified are met by the board. This approach may be more valid for two reasons.

First, board members can rarely stay adequately abreast of the status of all of the most important activities of the organization. And it may actually be less important that they do so than to ensure that their chief executive does. If a prominent funder asks a board member about the status of a program, most board members would be hard pressed to provide an up-to-date answer and would most likely respond in generalities. Just how much should the board be expected to know about the status of particular programs? Certainly board members might feel better if they are able to rattle off all the pertinent information, but in most cases it may be difficult to stay fully abreast of what is taking place in their organizations on an ongoing basis, except perhaps in a very small nonprofit organization.

However, the board can expect the executive director to provide periodic assessments of program status and accomplishment and reliable data that the board can use to determine how these programs are contributing to the accomplishment of the organization's mission. A board member can expect a chief executive to provide criteria for determining program effectiveness to the extent that objective criteria can be established. Many substantive tasks — redefining mission and programs, developing a strategic plan, approving budgets and policies, and obtaining the necessary resources — are the collaborative responsibility of the board and the executive. Though most authorities suggest that the board manage these tasks for itself, we agree with Paul Firstenberg's position: "Boards of trustees are essentially reactive — they work best when they can respond to presentations by management and are called upon to concur or disagree with quite specific proposals by the organization's executives. . . . In a sense, a board functions in an adjudicatory capacity" (1986, p. 204).

Second, keeping abreast of funding issues is a perplexing task for a board member. Often there are multiple funding sources, and each source may have its own form of accountability and record keeping. A small social service agency may have different contracts from city, county, state, and federal government agencies in addition to those from philanthropic sources. A large agency may have an even more complex revenue base. Staying abreast of these accounts and monitoring changes in them is a time-consuming and complicated matter.

We conclude that if a board does not undertake to carry out substantive tasks on its own, then the chief executive needs to initiate the processes necessary, gaining board approval for doing so. A board can make an informed judgment on the matter at hand if the chief executive is effective in facilitating its decision-making process. Once a strategic planning process, for example, is under way, the board's role will include participating in plan development, reviewing and perhaps modifying recommended plans, and finally officially approving them. The executive initiates action on these substantive board tasks; the board reacts to the tentative proposals or options developed by the executive (or other staff), perhaps leading the executive to develop modifications or alternative proposals; and finally the board approves a proposal that it understands and supports. A board can assess the effectiveness of its executive director in terms of how the executive facilitates this process.

The techniques a chief executive can use to facilitate the work of the board are many. For example, one of us serves as member of the board of a large nonprofit, nonpartisan citizen's league whose mission it is to identify, study, and make recommendations about significant issues facing our urban community. The organization has traditionally created and supported four or five ongoing task forces in various stages of work. A proposal was made by a segment of the board to dramatically alter the work of the organization by tying it to one major task study for a two-year period and finding $75,000 to do it. A lengthy board meeting was set aside to discuss this proposal. There was some indication prior to the meeting that the $75,000 might be available if the organization would shift the focus of its work. The executive director encouraged the board to spend the first thirty minutes of the meeting discussing the mission of the organization. A copy of the mission statement was made available for each board member. A lively discussion ensued.

Senior board members reminded newer board members about the recent and successful history of the organization. A founder of the organization and original drafter of the mission statement who had recently returned to the board provided a valuable interpretation of the mission statement in light of the proposal. The president made a short speech about the positive and negative aspects of redefining the mission of the organization in light of its past history and future funding prospects. The executive director played the valuable role of process consultant during the discussion by collecting board member comments on a flip chart, paraphrasing and repeating board member comments, and intervening when she felt one board member did not fully understand what another board member said.

The value of this preliminary discussion cannot be overemphasized. It set the tone and established a framework in which a thoughtful and thorough discussion of the proposal could occur. It allowed the board members an opportunity to reaffirm in a most positive way their commitment to the aims of the organization while tackling a fundamental organizational decision.

A second example is taken from an experience one of us had when serving as the president of a large academic association and accrediting body of graduate programs. The board of this association was involved in a strategic planning effort targeted at developing a five-year plan for the organization. A task force on the future of the organization had been appointed by the board, and the task force had met and taken testimony over a one-year period from association members. The work of the task force was completed when it submitted ten recommendations for the future of the organization to the board for its final review and approval. The report was explained to the board and some modifications were made to the recommendations. A second special session of the board was set aside to determine the priorities for the recommendations. Given the nature of the discussion at the first meeting, the board president and the task force chair anticipated the possibility of some conflict on the board over these priorities.

The executive director attended most of the task force meetings and provided staff support. The board president was able to attend only a few of the task force meetings but was apprised of the discussions by the executive director and task force chair after every meeting. The board was kept fully informed of the work of the task force through reports by the president and committee chair and memoranda prepared by the executive director.

As the deadline for the key priority meeting of the board approached, the president wanted to avoid open conflict on the board over priorities. It was important for the president that the board pull together and begin to implement the recommendations of the study as soon as possible. With a month remaining before the key board meeting, the president met with the executive director and jointly developed a plan of action including timely and strategic phone calls to key board members in order to smooth out any differences. The executive director made the bulk of the calls and put various members of the board in touch with other members to resolve differences.

When he believed most difficulties had been resolved, he prepared a letter for the president's signature that reflected the agreements that had been hammered out. Priorities were clearly identified. In effect, the executive director put the package together. The recommendations in the letter were passed unanimously. By working out the differences before the meeting, the executive director saved valuable board time and gave the board a chance to revel in the success of the strategic planning effort. The executive director sat quietly during the vote awaiting the most opportune moment to sketch out what he saw as the action plan and time lines needed to implement the plan.

These are two excellent examples of how especially effective chief executives work to effect the alternative model. There are other instances where board-centered leadership is most necessary. All organizations pass through critically important decisions or periods of extreme crisis when the very life of the organization may be at stake. Key fund-raising activities, the expansion of facilities, mergers, and the renegotiation, loss, or gain of large contracts are important transitions in an organization's life cycle and may dictate special involvement by the board and require the most thorough kind of board-centered leadership by the chief executive.

What are the circumstances that would result in a board's loss of faith in the judgment of the executive director? Apart from examples of gross mismanagement or unethical behavior, there are no clear-cut answers to this question. (We have found in our work only a few cases of chief executives who have made gross mistakes, and in every case we also found a board that was not actively involved in the organization.) The most critical times for board-centered leadership occur when events threaten the organization's very survival. It is at these times that leadership by the chief executive in energizing the board is most needed.

A board must be prepared to attend to the most important decisions facing the organization — and some of the most important decisions may be the most mundane. We are aware of cases when a board failed to ensure that an ordinary task such as filing taxes was handled properly. More than one nonprofit organization has folded for lack of funds to pay back taxes. It may be helpful for a board president and chief executive to prepare jointly an annual planning calendar noting when critical reports and filings are due.

In practice, boards carry out extremely important roles that complement the work of the chief executive. Establishing contacts, raising funds, enhancing the organization's reputation and giving it legitimacy, representing it publicly and politically, and giving it advice are among the examples that come to mind. The board reserves the right to review carefully any decision — especially those made during times of crisis or change — and can overturn any decision made by the chief executive.

Of course, we believe that effective executives will have worked carefully with their boards on the most important issues before any actions or final decisions are made. A successful chief executive never surprises the board and carefully works through issues that may upset the board. When the chief executive is unsure about how to proceed, the wise executive approaches the board with a full admission of uncertainty. Effective executives who practice the tenets of board-centered leadership should infrequently find themselves the subject of a negative evaluation by the board. Even more importantly, board-centered leadership furthers achieving the mission.

In the first three chapters we have described and diagnosed the sources and nature of the challenges of leadership in nonprofit organizations. Chapter One described the unique character and complex environment of nonprofit organizations, with special attention to how recent changes in government funding and regulation have affected programs and resources. A complex and changing environment makes for an open and dependent organization.

Chapter Two presented an analysis of nonprofit organizations as open systems subject to changing interests and expectations from a variety of constituencies or stakeholders. The unique character and highly open nature of nonprofit organizations mean that leadership in nonprofit organizations requires diverse skills as well as continuing adherence to guardianship of the public good. The leadership challenges are further complicated by the ambiguous roles and relations of chief executives and boards.

In this chapter we examine how the traditional model of nonprofit organizations, derived from the managed systems theory of organization, puts the board both at the top of the hierarchy of authority and at the center of leadership responsibility and leads to a set of heroic standards for board performance. Despite widespread acknowledgment of a persistent and often substantial gap between the heroic standards and reality, the traditional model remains preeminent. A more realistic alternative model is presented. It puts the chief executive at the center of leadership responsibility in nonprofit organizations and advocates that the executive engage in board-centered leadership. This model does not demote or disregard the board. Rather, it continues to see the board as critically important. However, the board is no longer expected to lead itself to meet its duties. When necessary, the effective chief executive takes responsibility for developing and leading the board. The next three chapters of this book will provide more detail about making this alternative model work.

FOUR

Key Leadership Strategies for Nonprofit Executives

●○○○

We have characterized nonprofit organizations as open systems with permeable boundaries affected significantly by factors in their environments. Leaders can exert some influence but little control over these factors. We have also suggested that nonprofit organizations are typically highly resource-dependent. The concept of resource dependence draws attention to the significant (and variable) extent to which an organization depends on outsiders for its survival. Imagine a medieval walled settlement in which hundreds of people live, including weavers, cobblers, bakers, blacksmiths, candlemakers, and so on. Also enclosed within the walls are fields and orchards. Such a settlement might be nearly self-sufficient, dependent on few others outside the walls for resources. Another, smaller settlement without fields and orchards inside its walls and lacking many craft skills among its members is much more dependent. Those living in this settlement will need to explore the environment outside, finding out who has the resources they need and negotiating exchanges with those individuals or groups.

Similarly, nonprofit organizations must monitor their environment and utilize exchanges with other organizations in the environment to garner the variety of required resources, including money, volunteers, clients, and legitimacy. Such exchanges occur with government and philanthropic interests as well as in the marketplace and are activated by economic, political, and moral relations. The task of managing these exchanges is what we have called creative boundary spanning, and it is the most fundamental element of leadership in nonprofit organizations.

The most clear-cut measure of a nonprofit organization's effectiveness is its survival. Survival is more likely when boundary-spanning activities secure sufficient resources for the organization and when its legitimacy is confirmed by society. Success is made possible by the maintenance of a regular flow of resources to the organization. This would be a simple problem if nonprofit organizations were in complete control of all the critical external components necessary for their operation. No nonprofit organization is so self-contained. Since the most critical resources are derived from the environment of the organization, every publicly supported charity must achieve some measure of legitimacy or social acceptance as a worthwhile and appropriate effort, and every such organization depends on others for financial support. Those with extensive government contracts or reliance upon a few large foundation grants are especially dependent. A most important measure of effectiveness of the leadership of these organizations has to do with how successfully this dependency is handled.

In our research on leadership in nonprofit organizations we found that chief executives play a crucial role in leadership beyond the organizational boundary as they deal with this dependency. It is a role different from that implied by the pyramidal description of the managed systems perspective that places the board in the principal position of responsibility for organizational outcomes. We have discovered that the major actors in nonprofit organizations — board presidents, staff, and chief executives alike — see the executive as responsible for the major outcomes in nonprofit organizations. All fingers of responsibility for critical events in the organization point to the chief executive, including his or her own.

However, chief executives are unlikely to act alone as they attempt to position their organizations in the environment. Our research, as reported in Chapter Three, shows that highly effective nonprofit executives work with and through their boards in leading their organizations. Thus, leadership across the boundary is a joint responsibility of the chief executive and the board. Experienced observers and practitioners — for example, Houle (1989) and O'Connell (1985) — argue that effective nonprofit organizations are those in which the board takes responsibility for success. Our studies suggest that success often depends on the chief executive's willingness and ability to enable the board to meet its responsibilities.

Often, analyses of organizational leadership concentrate almost exclusively on internal action. Other theories recognize that leadership is also an external process, though they have emphasized only very general concepts (for example, the importance of a vision, motivating communication, and so forth) or have treated leadership solely in organizational terms rather than breaking it down to analyze the behaviors of effective chief executives. For these reasons our analysis and suggestions draw heavily on the work of only a small number of other researchers and our own studies. In particular we have found the work of Huff (1985), Kotter (1982), and Dollinger (1984) especially useful. These sources suggest the following roles and strategies as important to effective leadership across the boundary.

The Need for an Integrative Function

Given the centrality of the chief executive to leadership in nonprofit organizations, he or she must usually act as a nerve center in actions taken both internally and externally. That is, the effective chief executive typically plays a central role in sensing the changing external environment and in developing and implementing, through the board, strategic responses to the external environment and adaptations in the internal operations of the organization. Many factors operate in an organization's environment and give rise to different ideas about how to deal with problems facing the organization. Board members have differing access to the environment and differing ideas and information about what the major issues are that face the organization. The executive is in a position to serve as the integrator and processor of these ideas and information.

The executive, as communication processor, serves as the focal point for information exchange. Individuals, groups, and organizations (the stakeholders of the organization) have many messages to exchange with each other. The messages vary in intelligibility and clarity and tell what each expects from and for the organization and what each will do in return if the non-profit organization meets certain expectations. The chief executive reads these messages and designs actions and creates new messages in response. However, messages from individuals or groups not heard from before sometimes arrive later than others, and revised or additional messages are slipped in by familiar figures. Thus, the executive must determine what messages require special attention, what messages need to be sent in return, and to what degree to adjust ongoing work in response to these messages. One of the executives in our study likened herself to "an operator at an old-fashioned switchboard." She explained, "If I position myself correctly between my board and my staff, between the major stakeholders in the community and my board, I am in the business of plugging communicators into other communicators. A principal aspect of my job is to facilitate the effective flow of information."

Attacking complex and ill-defined problems in the environment requires high levels of trust, strong board leadership, and, most importantly, a flow of information different from that in the traditional hierarchical model implied by the managed system definition. Different interests and ideas must be brought together in a spirit of consensus and shared direction. Unlike in the more traditional hierarchical model, the chief executive connects with and through the board to wide networks of interests and information affecting the organization to help create that sense of common understanding and shared direction.

The description of the executive as "communication processor" may not fully capture the often hectic, fragmented functions of the chief executive. A telephone exchange certainly acts more efficiently and smoothly than can the chief executive in response to the many incoming and outgoing messages. The chaotic and often uncertain nature of these messages means that the executive expends much effort managing contradictions. In the reality of organizational life, the chief executive is responsible for the major activities of the organization and is held accountable for major events that affect the organization, yet the board is expected to be in charge. The traditional managed systems perspective we critique in Chapter Three describes the organization as indisputably hierarchical, but most effective executives spend a majority of their time coping with external relations, adjusting policies, and realigning resources. Such actions may accumulate in a redefinition of mission — a role prescribed for the board in the traditional model.

Spend Time on External Relations

Like other executives, nonprofit chief executives work long hours. There are many demands on their time. Many of these demands arise in the routine activities and inevitable day-to-day problems of the internal operations of the organization. These activities can easily absorb much of a chief executive's time. Dollinger's (1984) research on small business owners and managers finds that resisting such nearly exclusive attention to internal matters importantly related to success. He found that those owners and managers who spent more time on boundary-spanning or external activities were more successful. Similarly, the especially effective nonprofit chief executives in our studies often emphasized the importance of maintaining, strengthening, and expanding their connections with external interests.

Obviously, spending more time on external matters means spending less time on internal affairs. For many nonprofit chief executives, spending time externally has required the development of more decentralized internal management and has called for delegating more authority and responsibility to staff. As one of the executives in our study said, "You can't work in the community if your staff can't mind the shop."

Delegating to others is one of the most basic and important management processes in organizations. Without delegation by the chief executive to the staff, no nonprofit organization can function effectively. The courage to delegate properly involves risk, and the knowledge of how to do so is difficult to come by. There are no hard and fast rules to follow. Inadequate or improper delegation may be the cause of many failures in nonprofit organizations.

Almost all delegation to staff can be thought of as occurring in the context of decision making. Executives must decide when they should make a decision by themselves and when to involve their staff. Some actions can or must be delegated totally to staff. Thus, it is helpful to think of delegation as the executive's trust of a subordinate to make a high-quality decision. Certainly trust of one's subordinates increases as they acquire experience in handling problems. Subordinates' abilities to handle more complex and difficult decisions is directly related to their current competencies and to the time the executive spends in their training and development.

A key to successful delegation is to be found in the quality of staff hired and the time spent in enhancing the skills and abilities of subordinates by increasing their sense of confidence and competence. Delegating makes subordinates feel essential to the organization. Feeling essential to the organization increases the willingness of a subordinate to accept greater responsibility. Thus, success in the boundary-spanning role is directly related to successful delegation, which in turn derives from the effective development of the human resources in the organization.

"I learned to manage an agency like this one," one of our effective executives reported, "from my former boss, who was around only when we needed her. She trusted me to make good judgments, and if I didn't, she helped me learn from my mistakes. She was usually busy out working the community, but she always had time to help me if I had questions. It wasn't long before she just left me alone. I knew about all there was to know about how to deliver our programs. Now that I am a chief executive, I manage this agency the same way."

Spending less time on managing internal functions may seem contradictory to some executives who have major concerns about the administrative efficiencies of their organizations. We believe these contradictions are a necessary part of the work of the nonprofit chief executive. For example, subordinates need to be given a clear understanding of their jobs and their scope; job descriptions can and should be written. Yet most jobs in nonprofit organizations overlap. Subordinates must understand the underlying continuity of their job in an organization plagued by environmental uncertainty and change. Encouraging clearly scheduled and logically planned workdays for subordinates is apparently inconsistent with the often impromptu contacts and the jumping from issue to issue that characterize the typical day. Yet scheduling and planning provide a stable structure from which the exceptional can be more adequately handled. Executives need to break down larger tasks into explicit goals and subgoals, while recognizing that most important problems flow through the organization without an opportunity to neatly package them or solve them once and for all. In a world of shifting problems and priorities, spending too much time trying to rationalize most nonprofit organizations is futile. Only those tasks that are stable can be arranged as logical and routine processes. This framework establishes a basis for responding to the exceptions and new opportunities.

We do not know what proportion of time effective nonprofit chief executives devote to boundary spanning compared to managing the internal operations of the organization. The ratio will be affected by such factors as the size of the organization and the extent of its resource dependence. We believe, however, that the marginal payoff of spending more time across the boundary would be significant for most chief executives. An admonition to spend more time on external relations, of course, does not provide any guidance about where or on what to use the time. The next section offers some clues on that score.

Develop an Informal Information Network

Over the last decade major corporations bought into the idea that comprehensive and formal (typically computerized) management information systems were essential to the work of senior managers. Ideas about how to develop and manage these systems were to be found extensively (and still are) in the management literature, and at significant effort and cost these systems have been installed and maintained. The rationale for comprehensive information systems, consistent with the classical managed systems view, is that in a hierarchical arrangement those at the top need to receive all the available and important information necessary to make critical decisions. Excitement about the potential of these systems was fueled by increasing technical sophistication in information storage and retrieval.

However, as these systems grow in size and complexity it has become increasingly clear that comprehensive information systems are not working as planned. Senior managers are just not using them as their designers assumed. Research by Henry Mintzberg (1973) sheds light on why. He concludes from his studies of corporate executives that there are clear reasons for the waning interest in these systems. Simply put, there seems to be a strong preference by managers for verbal media—namely meetings and interpersonal contacts. Senior managers seem to value soft information over hard. Soft information includes gossip, hearsay, and even wild speculation captured in the here and now of primarily face-to-face encounters.

Mintzberg suggests a number of reasons for this preference. Aggregate hard information, delivered by management information systems, is always historical. Nor does hard information always lend itself well to the two prime uses managers have for information: to identify problems and opportunities and to construct a mental image of what is going on—how changes in external events may be affecting the organization, how the organization's environment may be changing, how the budget may look in the next year, how clients really feel about a service, and so on. Effective managers, Mintzberg suggests, piece together tidbits of information from many sources and build their own models to use in analyzing problems and predicting outcomes.

Mintzberg (1975) uses an observation by Richard Neustadt, who examined the way that Presidents Roosevelt, Truman, and Eisenhower collected information, to help make his point: "It is not information of a general sort that helps a President see personal stakes; not summaries, not surveys, not the bland amalgams. Rather . . . it is the odds and ends of tangible detail that pieced together in his mind illuminate the underside of issues put before him. To help himself he must reach out as widely as he can for every scrap of fact, opinion, gossip, bearing on his interests and relationships as President. He must become his own director of his own intelligence" (p. 52).

Although Mintzberg's arguments are based upon his studies of corporate executives, the way that they collected and processed information also characterizes the efforts of effective nonprofit executives.

The reality of organizational life for the nonprofit executive is that work is often at odds with the assumptions of the rational, managed systems perspective. Although most nonprofit executives might prefer a fairly orderly, compartmentalized world of predictable goals, easily identifiable resources, and unambiguous performance measures, they find just the opposite. Instead of making big decisions in the context of full information and in an orderly way, nonprofit executives must face the reality of partial information, quick compromise, and incomplete negotiation.

In addition, time must regularly be spent on relationships in a broadly based information network. This requires extraordinary patience and perseverance, because much of the time is spent with different people in a never-ending series of contacts. Effective executives must listen and plead, argue and help, cajole and wait. They must attend meetings and lunches, breakfasts and legislative sessions. This method of developing relationships to acquire intelligence and press their interests is at the core of their work.

Important, useful information is more likely to flow when the parties are more than acquaintances. The effectiveness of face-to-face communications is well known, and direct contacts are to be preferred. Some degree of reciprocal trust and credibility must be developed and maintained, and nothing helps more to create and maintain trust than firsthand opportunities to communicate. Although valuable information can be acquired from sources that are impersonal (for example, newsletters, budget information, minutes of meetings, intelligence about grant proposals and copies of such proposals, and so forth), the value of firsthand, face-to-face communication cannot be overstated. As a consequence it is important that an executive know how and with whom to quickly establish good working relationships. Receptions before professional meetings, casual invitations for lunch, and memberships in a wide circle of associations all provide such opportunities.

Attempting to develop such networks without some degree of trust is manipulative. A successful network is built and sustained when one is willing and able to understand and accept the interests of others, and it requires exchanging reliable information, without the violation of another's confidentiality. It means not only investing time but also helping others with their concerns in exchange for help with your own. Investing time to develop trusting relationships has payoff beyond ensuring that one's information is valid or that one's attempts to influence others will be accepted. The investment increases one's legitimacy as a valuable and contributing member of the nonprofit community.

Both Kotter's (1982) study of corporate general managers and Huff's (1985) study of school superintendents highlight the significant extent to which managers cultivate external sources of information. As Huff notes, a network is important for more than conveying information. Networks also are crucially involved in making sense of an often rapidly changing field. Different kinds of information are available from different parts of the environment of an organization. Information gleaned from membership in a professional association will be different from information collected from involvement in a local service club. Both can be important to a particular policy issue or service concern. The network, as a collectivity, has an important role in defining emerging issues and in pointing the way toward new program practices. A chief executive who is active in a variety of networks is both more likely to have some impact on the direction of the field that is of interest to that network and in a better position to make sense of the changing environment for others, including board members and staff. A leadership role in a network provides special access to information from or influence on the network.

Nonprofit organizations and their chief executives, of course, are usually a part of more than one field. For example, a local organization providing emergency assistance to the poor is part of the national, state, and local fields concerned with homelessness, hunger, and employment. The organization may also be part of a religious body, part of a United Way, and part of a coalition of inner city agencies. The networks associated with all these fields may to a greater or lesser extent overlap. A chief executive with strong connections in all these networks is in an unique position to make sense of what's happening in the various fields and use that information to advance the organization's mission. In our work with nonprofit executives we find the same group of executives involved in the leadership of local nonprofit organization associations, involved in the local chapters of public executive associations, involved in statewide advocacy groups, and so on. Many of the same faces show up at different kinds of meetings, in different parts of our community. And not by chance, the faces most familiar are those of executives who come from the most visible, effective, and well supported nonprofit organizations.

One last consideration about the conditions for determining whether one's involvement in a network may be helpful. It seems so basic as to be axiomatic: Without reliable information, an executive cannot act effectively on behalf of the organization. There are many ways to check the validity of information, particularly if one has membership in many different networks and has access to lots of people. Yet the final judgment about the validity of the information collected is the executive's. The strategic information system of the boundary-spanning executive is in the executive's mind, not in a computer. Important information comes in verbal form and must be collected and synthesized by the executive.

We suspect that because effective executives have learned how to process all the necessary information, they often find it difficult to tell someone else all that that person needs to know to make good decisions. It may seem easier for the manager to make the decision than to delegate it. This reality, and the complexity of many of the most important problems faced in the environment, may help explain why so many fingers of responsibility point to the chief executive for the most critical decisions facing nonprofit organizations and why the process of delegation by chief executives is so difficult in many nonprofit organizations.

Know Your Agenda

For some years now, strategic planning has been a hot topic in nonprofit management. More and more nonprofit organizations have undertaken formal planning processes. The process and outcomes of strategic planning serve many uses for a nonprofit organization (see Bryson, 1988, for a useful guide) and its chief executive. The formal plan, of course, provides the organization's leaders with fundamental goals and strategies; the plan frames the organization's agenda. Both Kotter (1982) and Huff (1985) find that executives also often develop and use agendas that are both more immediate and more long-range. However developed, a short list of goals or outcomes (typically no more than two, three, or occasionally four) is crucial to provide focus for the executive's work and substance for participation in networks.

The myriad activities and small-scale problems that pull chief executives in many different directions constantly threaten to turn their work into directionless reactivity. Knowing and using the agenda to focus work offers a basis for effectively allocating time and effort. A limited, focused agenda and the strategies for advancing it help to manage a complex and rapidly changing environment. Keeping the agenda in the forefront also permits the chief executive to use interactions with others to advance the agenda. Huff (1985) has described three strategies effective executives often employ in advancing their agenda as: dramatizing events related to the agenda, "laying a bread crumb trail," and simplifying.

Dramatizing events entails calling attention to the relationship between networking events and the executive's agenda. For example, an executive who wants to add staff fluent in Spanish to expand services to Spanish-speaking communities might send clippings about growth in the city's Latino population and its service problems to board members. The executive might also feature a digest of such stories in the organization's newsletter and see that the newsletter goes to regular funders. The key is to dramatically or memorably connect public issues to the organization's agenda.

Another good example of how to dramatize events comes from the chief executive of an agency serving the developmentally disabled. She encouraged a friend who taught creative writing at a local university to engage a class in developing a story about a day in the life of her agency. The story was included in the materials made available to those attending an annual banquet and awards dinner for the organization. The story was presented to the many stakeholders and others to give them a "real feel for the work of the agency." Clearly, the executive director had additional uses for the story. The description skillfully catalogued the creative work of a staff constrained by limited resources. Copies of the story became part of the publicity program of the agency and were conveniently included in reports to funders and in grant applications.

Just as dramatizing external events is a way of focusing attention, so too is the "laying of a bread crumb trail." Over time, through various communications, a chief executive points the way to an important decision. As Huff (1985, p. 175) puts it, organizational action requires that an executive edit his or her concerns "into a smaller number of items that can be comprehended by others. Repetition of these concerns is almost always necessary to gain the attention of others and convince them of serious intent." Such a strategy is probably widely applicable, but we find it especially germane in executive-board relations.

Consider, for instance, the strategy of the chief executive of an organization that operates group homes for the mentally ill. The organization's original facility, called Tracy House, was an old building in great need of repair. Operations at the house did not quite break even. Surpluses from the operation of other facilities covered the shortfall. The executive, based on what he was hearing from the network of licensing, funding,

and accrediting bodies, believed that new standards would require modifications that, combined with no growth in state daily
rates, would mean operating the facility at an increasing deficit.
So he began laying out a bread crumb trail for board members,
both formally in board meetings and informally in conversations in other settings. Part of his problem was that a few board
members had a strong emotional attachment to Tracy House;
they had personally painted it and made repairs to meet licensing standards. Instead of pointing out over and over again that
the Tracy House was decrepit, he provided an update on the
state funding prospects, noting the financial implications for each
facility, which made the burden of carrying the home's deficit
obvious. Some time later, he mentioned the possibility of federal housing funds becoming available for group home construc-
tion, observing that this would permit the organization to "get
out from under" Tracy House. In this way, when the decision
was finally taken to sell Tracy House, it was a foregone conclusion. The trail of markers not only defined and focused the issue, it also brought everyone to the same conclusion, making
what could have been a painful decision easy.

The last strategy identified by Huff is to keep things as
simple as possible. A complex and interdependent world en-
hances the tendency for inaction and drift. Before we can make
a decision about X, we have to see what happens with Y, and
Y depends on what A and B do. To make decisions and take
action, individuals must risk simplifying the situation. As Huff
(1985) observes, behaving as though the situation is simpler than
you know it to be helps bring about more simplicity. Acting
in relation to the agenda is an important way of simplifying,
or creating order in a disorderly world.

Improvise; Accept Multiple, Partial Solutions

The point of leadership across the boundary is to position the
organization in the larger environment and match its capabilities with the demands for its services and the resources available. Of course, the inevitable fact is that neither organizational
capabilities nor environmental demands and resources are static.

A short, clear agenda and the strategies for implementing it provide a compass pointing the way to where the executive, who has integrated to the greatest extent possible the preferences of the stakeholders, wants to go.

The metaphor of the compass, however, is not entirely complete because the executive (reflecting the stakeholders' varying preferences) wants to go to several places. For example, the agenda might include increasing total revenues as well as diversifying revenue sources, acquiring a new facility, and expanding a particular program. Not only are these different goals, but there are likely to be different paths to each. Furthermore, the most direct path to one may make paths to the others longer or more difficult to find. Finding the combination of paths that most efficiently leads to all three goals may often be beyond calculation, particularly when the environment keeps changing. The upshot is that executives must sometimes be willing and able to improvise, to take an unexpected path when it presents itself.

Sometimes chief executives find they cannot, at least within a crucial time period, reach a goal in exactly the form imagined. As Huff (1985, p. 167) observes, an "administrator's ability to perceive issues is almost always bigger than the ability to act on issues. As a result, the administrator often must be content to work on a small part of the larger whole." That is, sometimes the organization may have to go someplace a little different from what was at one time imagined because that's where the only available path leads. Huff (p. 168) further suggests that a "specific action should rarely be taken unless it is compatible with several different issues." Or, in the terms of our metaphor, an action that leads to movement on paths to two or three places at once is particularly useful.

For an especially compelling illustration of this sort of creative leadership, let us look at the case of a nonprofit organization that required a facility with large spaces. For several years the organization used an old warehouse that a business corporation provided free. However, the corporation made clear that it was interested in selling the warehouse and that the organization might have to relocate. As a few years passed and the corporation had no success in selling the warehouse and little apparent necessity for doing so, the issue of obtaining a suitable, more permanent facility was increasingly put on the back burner. One day the chief executive received a call from a corporate officer saying that a tentative agreement to sell the warehouse had been reached and that the organization would have to vacate in six months. The first thing the chief executive did was to call the board. Staff were also quickly informed so as to avoid the spread of rumors. The chief executive found that many board members and staff assumed that the organization should try to find another old warehouse. However, the executive knew that old warehouses had several disadvantages: high energy costs, lack of parking, inaccessibility, and so forth. The executive thought this was an excellent opportunity to rethink what sort of facility would be most appropriate.

After conferring with the board chairman and other key board members, a facility planning committee was formed. The executive was interested in connecting the facility issue to other agenda issues, especially those of enhancing collaboration with other community organizations and adding a demonstration day care program for children. As the facility planning committee identified alternative ways of securing a replacement facility and the costs associated with each, a board member suggested the executive meet with an official from a local community college. While the community college was not in the same service field as the organization, the community college had enough money available through a bond issue to construct a new building, but not enough money to fully finish and equip the building. Following quick negotiations the organization agreed to provide funds to finish and equip the facility in exchange for a ten-year lease of two floors at a very low rental rate. This solution, though not perfect, moved the organization along on several agenda issues simultaneously. This progress was achieved because the executive worked with and through the board and linked action on one issue with progress on others.

Developing a Powerful Board

A common, if only sometimes successful, strategy to improve a nonprofit organization's position in its environment is that of developing a "power board." A power board is one that includes some of the community's social, economic, and political elite. In some communities the social and economic elite are the same people.

A publication from a fund-raising consulting firm makes the case for a power board very clear: "[The] name of the game is *power* — power to act, influence, lead, advocate, support and communicate. An organization must have trustees who can *get things done,* on their own and through others. It doesn't hurt if the board is 'representative' of the community, and if its members like one another personally. But these conditions aren't essential to an effective board. Power is" (Goettler Associates, 1986, p. 7).

Whether a nonprofit organization should or can pursue the strategy of developing a powerful board is an open question. The reduction in government funding for a variety of nonprofit programs had led to an increased emphasis on private donations. This emphasis on greater private giving in turn often leads to attempts to develop a power board. To help address the issues surrounding the creation of a powerful board, an explanation of how such boards are developed and maintained may be helpful.

Galaskiewicz's (1985) study of business-nonprofit relations in Minneapolis–St. Paul clearly demonstrates the importance of social exchanges in the relationship between the nonprofit organization and the elite board. In every community there is a hierarchy of nonprofit, charitable organizations such that board membership confers more or less social prestige. In most communities the symphony orchestra, the major museums, and certain private colleges and universities sit at the pinnacle of this prestige hierarchy, with other nonprofit organizations arrayed further down. As Galaskiewicz shows, the nonprofit organizations at the top offer board members prestige and participation in the highest circles of the civic culture. In exchange, the board members provide contributions from their businesses, personal gifts, and active solicitation of others connected to them. Thus, board membership of the social and business elite brings legitimacy, connections, and money.

Nonprofit prestige hierarchies are not immutable. Organizations at the top must continue to attract those powerful board members, who will in turn attract others. Some nonprofit organizations that occupy middling levels in the hierarchy try to find ways of moving up the ladder by recruiting one or two well-connected board members or those they believe will soon be among the community's elite. The dynamics can be likened to a multi-group dance. At the start, one group of dancers has several members with high prestige and power. Other individuals try to get noticed by this group or offer to participate in some preliminary (training) dances with them. Some who are part of the high prestige group are asked to dance with other, less prestigious groups. When these two processes are in full swing, the dance floor may be the scene of rapidly changing groups. By the time the ball is over, most groups maintain their original membership and relative prestige while a few change positions slightly. Many nonprofit organizations never participate in this "prestige dance," either because directors and staff find doing so inconsistent with personal or organizational values or because the nature of the organization's purposes, services, and constituencies makes effectively doing so unlikely.

Should a nonprofit organization pursue a power board strategy? Our personal views are that there is nothing inherently objectionable in attempting to add prestigious, powerful, or wealthy people to a board, so long as such individuals are willing to meet the expectations that apply to other board members. Current directors and the chief executive must expect developing such a board to be difficult and slow. Few board members want to change groups.

Though we have no systematic evidence for it, our impression is that nonprofit organizations that do not explicitly set out to attract more powerful boards, but rather set out to improve the performance of their existing boards, are likely to develop more effective boards. That is, nonprofit organizations that take steps to improve board member recruitment, selection, training, and performance are more likely to develop effective, hard-working boards than those that directly seek to add the powerful. A strategy of pursuing an active, hard-working board rather than an elite one is, we believe, both more realistic for the great majority of nonprofit organizations and more likely to lead to success. Most of the elite in a community are familiar with success, and one good way to attract the elite is to become a highly successful organization bent upon even greater success.

Developing a "Political Strategy"

All nonprofit organizations are affected by and involved in politics, broadly conceived. If we think of politics as issues of who gets what, why, and how, as issues of what a society should provide as rights and what as marketplace goods, and as processes for deciding such issues, then all nonprofit organizations are inevitably part of the political process. Even if we think of politics more narrowly, as involving issues of who is elected and what laws are passed, almost all nonprofit organizations remain part of the political process. What political strategies should nonprofit organizations pursue as they attempt to improve their positions in the environment?

Federal, as well as state and local, laws restrict the political activities of nonprofit organizations. Because nonprofit organizations receive benefits from the government that other private organizations do not, their participation in politics has been limited to a geater extent than that of other private organizations (see Simon, 1987, for an overview of the legal and tax status of nonprofit organizations). The restrictions on political activities vary depending on the type of nonprofit organization. Following Simon's (1987) classification, there are four types of nonprofit organizations: (1) those that are not included in section 501(c)(3) of the Internal Revenue Code, including trade and professional associations, labor unions, and Chambers of Commerce, which are all exempt from corporate income tax but are not usually eligible for tax-deductible gifts from individuals, (2) the 501(c)(3) publicly supported charitable organizations, (3) the 501(c)(3) operating foundations, and (4) the 501 (c)(3) grant-making foundations.

All three classes of 501(c)(3) organizations are prohibited from campaigning for or against the election of candidates to political office. The non-501(c)(3) nonprofit organizations may engage in electoral politics. They are also permitted to participate in legislative advocacy, that is, lobbying. Operating and grant-making foundations are prohibited from legislative lobbying, except in very specific circumstances. The rules affecting lobbying by 501(c)(3) publicly supported charities have long been vague and uncertain. In 1934 a provision was added to the tax laws specifying that "no substantial part" of the activities of nonprofit charitable organizations may constitute "carrying on propaganda, or otherwise attempting to influence legislation."

The courts have avoided defining "substantial" in any absolute or percentage terms, relying on the extent of legislative activities in the context of other objectives and circumstances. Many observers believe that the vagueness of this standard has deterred many nonprofit organizations from any involvement in legislative issues. To provide more useful guidelines, Congress enacted, as part of the 1976 Tax Reform Act, procedures through which nonprofit charitable organizations may choose ("elect," in the terms of tax law) to be subject to specific percentage limitations on legislative expenditures rather than the usual "no substantial part" rule. Those organizations that so elect may spend 20 percent of their first $500,000 of exempt-purposes expenditures (usually, all expenditures except fund-raising expenditures) on activities directed at influencing legislation, 15 percent of the next $500,000 of exempt-purposes expenditures, 10 percent of the next $500,000, and 5 percent of any remaining expenditures, up to a limit of $1 million per year. However, no more than 25 percent of lobbying expenditures may be devoted to grass-roots lobbying (that is, to influencing the general public on legislative matters).

Late in 1986 the Department of the Treasury issued more detailed proposals for implementing the elective rules. The proposed rules dealt extensively with defining the expenditures that would establish the base to which the lobbying percentages would apply; with defining what expenditures are lobbying and grassroots lobbying; and with defining accounting rules for allocating "mixed purpose" expenditures. The proposed rules were widely perceived as hostile to the nonprofit sector, and a substantial campaign, led by Independent Sector (a coalition of national nonprofit organizations, foundations, and corporate giving programs), was mounted to challenge the proposals. The effort was successful to the extent that the Internal Revenue Service proposed less restrictive regulations late in 1988. Final regulations are expected by the end of 1990.

The implication of this legal overview is simply that charitable nonprofit organizations can legitimately participate in political and legislative processes (except elections). What political strategies should leaders of nonprofit organizations pursue? It seems to us there are four broad kinds of strategies that can be usefully pursued. The first of these is efforts directed at shaping public opinion. Though not usually considered political in the narrower sense of the specific laws, public opinion, particularly as it comes to be communicated to legislators and policymakers, is often crucial for nonprofit organizations. As some social condition comes to be perceived as a problem that deserves public attention (for example, domestic violence or homelessness), then some nonprofit organizations can present themselves as vehicles for ameliorating the problem. Organizations can get their causes into the public opinion arena by communicating with their constituencies, with potentially sympathetic groups, and with the mass media. Such communications may take the form of newsletters, speakers' bureaus, press releases, and the like. Every organization needs to get its story heard. Of course, board members and other volunteers are especially effective public advocates since their efforts are less likely to be perceived as self-interested and since they may have access to opinion leaders.

A second political strategy is an extension of the more general strategy of developing informal information networks. Specifically, the strategy is to develop and maintain networks with governmental administrators and elected officials. Effective use of this strategy involves not only the chief executive's network, but the networks of other staff and board members. If a chief executive is aware of others' networks, then he or she can get alternative perspectives on events or likely events as well as discover unexpected paths to goals.

A third strategy is to pursue legislation. Compared to other participants in legislative politics, most nonprofit organizations are distinctly disadvantaged. As organizations they cannot contribute to candidates. They seldom can credibly claim to influence many voters. Their chief assets in legislative arenas are accurate information, moral authority, and a willingness to work in coalition with others. In an age in which public attitudes about politicians and the political process have become, understandably, highly cynical, these tools may seem puny and out-of-date. Nonetheless, we believe that not only are these tools all that many nonprofit organizations are ever likely to have, they are also ethically enough. Though it may seem naive to practitioners of *realpolitik,* we think nonprofit organizations that engage in questionable practices (anything they wouldn't be willing to make public) not only put themselves at risk but also put the entire nonprofit sector at risk.

A fourth strategy, including political officials on the board, is a variant of the power board strategy. As such, the same questions of which nonprofit organizations can attract which political officials and in exchange for what remain relevant. The inclusion of elected officials on boards raises additional issues. The experience of most nonprofit organizations is that such members are usually not very active in the work of the board. Given the many demands on their time, it is not surprising that they infrequently attend meetings or take on other tasks. What effect will this minimal participation have on the work of other members? Will having such special-case board members be regarded as inequitable? How will others in the community, including foundations and corporate donors, perceive the addition of an elected official? Will including an elected official displease supporters of that official's political opponents, who may then withdraw support from the nonprofit organization if the official is turned out of office? Finally, what can a nonprofit organization reasonably expect elected officials to do? They may not be able or willing to deliver as much as anticipated.

Some have argued that including elected officials on boards is inherently unethical since the obvious rationale is to gain an advantage over others in seeking funding and other favorable governmental action. The goal is to tilt the political process, to achieve a presumably unfair advantage. This is an important argument that deserves serious treatment. Like everyone else, we do not oppose fair process. However, especially in legislative and governmental processes, what are the standards of fairness? Is it unfair to have proposed legislation introduced that would increase state funding for drug treatment when there are many other deserving uses for limited funds? Is it unfair to ask a legislator (one on your board, who might be easier to reach and more likely to respond) to inquire of state departmental staff how an application is faring? We accept that unequal access to legislators can lead to unfair processes, but we argue that such is not inevitable. We expect that nonprofit leaders will be acutely sensitive to these sticky ethical issues.

In summary, it is necessary but insufficient for a chief executive to be concerned primarily with the efficient internal operations of the organization. Effective nonprofit chief executives need to influence people and systems beyond the boundaries of their organization. An extensive array of contacts may include those in government agencies, foundations, accrediting bodies, professional associations, similar nonprofit organizations, and other influential groups.

As chief executives spend more time working across boundaries, many skills become essential, including those of negotiation and conflict resolution, delegation, building trust, gaining intelligence, and network building. Executives must understand the character and motives of people in the cross-boundary worlds with whom they deal — the press, legislators, corporate executives, lobbyists, community leaders, and others. They must have an intimate understanding of the needs, interests, talents, and commitment of members of their board and skill in developing the kind of board that will know how to collectively advance the interests of the organization. The skills necessary for the chief executive to function as the integrator, the developer, and the sustainer of the board form the subject of Chapter Five.

FIVE

Engaging and Developing
The Board

●○○○

Shifts in funding sources and amounts, changes in political priorities and players, and turnover in the composition and interests
of stakeholders are among many factors that require ongoing
response and adaptation by the leaders of nonprofit organizations. In Chapter Four we described the importance of chief
executive leadership across the boundary of the organization
to deal with environmental exigencies that may affect the organization. In this chapter we refine our discussions to describe
more particularly how the chief executive can work to ensure
that the board is prepared to respond effectively to problems
and opportunities created by changes in the environment. Our
research shows that the primary behaviors that characterize effective chief executives are those associated with board-centered
leadership, and we believe that the most effective chief executives engage their boards in special ways to see that they are
ready and able to deal effectively with externally induced challenges.

Given that the board has ultimate hierarchical authority
and is the executive's boss, though seldom the center of leadership responsibility, what might executives do to help develop
a board fully prepared to respond to challenges and opportunities? As there are multiple ways in which boards may fall short

of meeting their responsibilities, an important first step for a chief executive is to assess the board's performance and analyze the likely reasons for any shortcomings. Distinguishing the symptoms from the causes of poor board performance is crucial. Developing the skills of effective diagnosis is a good starting point for an executive director who wants to become adept at making this distinction.

Understanding the Board at Work

Most board meetings are busy affairs. The chief executive is usually engaged fully in the business at hand — working through an agenda, dealing with requests for information, making reports, and so on. However, if the executive disengages momentarily from these tasks, it is possible to observe much going on. One discovers who is talking to whom on the board, who is silent, and perhaps why. One notices who has bought into a decision and who may have been cut out. One begins to observe how certain board members line up on a position and what is happening to the rest of the board as a result.

There are many symptoms of deficient board performance, some more obvious than others. Some board members are actively involved; others contribute very little. Little or no preparation for meetings, unwillingness to accept task assignments, incomplete or inadequate follow-through on assignments, and unresolved differences, conflict, or factions on the board are all symptoms of major underlying problems.

Symptoms are manifested in other ways. It is unrealistic to expect 100 percent attendance at every board or committee meeting. Busy people will have other claims on their time. But if meetings have been scheduled well in advance with attention to confirming the availability of those expected to attend and materials (including the agenda) have been sent several days prior to the meeting and yet several members fail to attend, clearly there's a problem. Or if the meetings are a series of motions with little or no discussion prior to approvals, then they have become purely ritualistic. These symptoms of poor board performance have their source in more fundamental problems, and it is the problems, not the symptoms, that need to be addressed. Trying to correct symptoms deflects energies that are better directed at solving the problem. Careful observation of the board at work may shed light on the symptoms but may not tell us much about the underlying problem.

The causes of problems on boards are found in the ongoing activities of a board; how goals are set, what role individual board members play in setting those goals, how an individual board member's interests and needs are met, how patterns of influence and control on the board evolve. It is important to realize that problems unfold over time because the board is an ongoing system of social interaction. To understand this process, it is helpful to distinguish between the substantive things that are dealt with at a manifest level (for example, what is talked about) and the latent activities that underlie the process (for example, who is participating, who is not, and why).

When a board engages in an argument, for instance, the subject under discussion is the substantive, concrete matter at stake. However, as many have observed, the real conflict or disagreement is often about something other than what is nominally at issue. Effective conflict resolution often requires that the disagreement be reframed or understood at different levels of analysis.

For instance, Terry (1981) has suggested that organizational disagreements can be hierarchically classified as about: (1) resources, (2) structures and procedures, (3) power, and (4) purposes. He asserts that disputes nominally about resources are really about structures and procedures for allocating or attracting resources; that disputes about procedures are really about power; and that conflicts about power are truly differences in purpose. Expressed conflict at one level may best be resolved by moving to the next level to reach agreement. According to this scheme, the ultimate way to resolve conflict is to reach agreement on purposes.

We are not sure that the hierarchical arrangement of issues holds for everyone or that agreement on purposes provides an adequate basis for effectively resolving all intra-organizational conflicts. However, the more general point — that disagreements are usually expressed in terms not fully revealing of the real source of the disagreement — is clearly useful. The process of board work must also be understood at the latent level of the board's interaction. Differences among board members may find their root in a lack of shared direction or perhaps in changes in direction required by external events that some board members may not fully understand.

Diagnostic skill involves the ability to see a board at work as a whole in all its complexity. Diagnostic skill also means understanding with great sensitivity individual board members' interests and needs. It includes recognizing how various board members depend on each other and how changes in one individual's behavior affect others. It includes recognizing how the actions of certain board members add to or detract from the overall effectiveness of the board. In short, developing diagnostic skill means two things: being aware of how the board as a group does its work in accomplishing its goals, and understanding the needs and wants of individual board members as they define their role on the board.

These two fundamental issues — the clarity of the organizational mission and board members' role expectations — significantly influence the effectiveness of the board as a whole and the level of commitment and motivation of individual board members. All boards must deal successfully with these two issues if they are to be effective.

Clarity of Organizational Mission

For a board to run effectively, individual members must have a shared definition of the organization's mission — its reason to function as an organization. Conflicts over priorities of direction must be understood, addressed, and resolved by a board if the mission of the organization is to be achieved. In the absence of clarity in mission, it is not surprising to find either a board on which members may be working hard but pulling in different directions or a board not working very hard at all because individual board members do not know which way to direct their efforts.

Clarifying the mission of the organization requires ongoing attention because the environment of most nonprofit organizations is continually changing. Many effective boards devote much thought and time to defining the purpose of the organization, only to find that external events make a redefinition or refinement of the mission necessary. At one level it may be helpful for a mission to be broadly enough conceived to capture in the most comprehensive way what the organization is about and thus allow modifications in programs to occur without a significant change in mission. On another level, the mission and its requirements should be understood with enough specificity to help focus the board on the major activities in which the organization must engage. It should define the fundamental strategies that are needed for the organization to attain its goals. An example of the importance of this distinction can be found in a major conflict that took place on a board that did not agree about its fundamental mission.

A nonprofit trolley company was founded primarily to provide a regular transport service for tourists, connecting specific places of interest in the city. The board of the company found itself split over the issue of whether the company should apply for a Department of Transportation grant that would provide safety training for its drivers. Both the president of the board and the executive director advocated seeking the grant and had been told by the department that it would be receptive to an application. A second opportunity to obtain government funds was presented to the board by a suburban city that was willing to pay for a subsidized extension of operations beyond the existing service area to an important tourist site in the suburb. The offer from the suburban city meant not only government subsidization of another kind but an exciting opportunity for major growth in the services of the company.

The president and chief executive, who both embraced these two opportunities, began preparing the grant application and started initial negotiations with the suburban city. They were then confronted by two powerful founding board members who were concerned that these two opportunities would lead to a significant change in "the philosophy of the company," as they put it. A board retreat was called by the president and chief executive.

It became clear at the retreat that the board disagreed significantly about what it meant to provide public transport service and the extent to which the company could or should be supported by public funds. At the most fundamental level there were differences in the basic definition of the mission of the organization. One of the founding board members argued that it was not by accident that they called themselves "a company." It was intended from the beginning that the company be operated "solely from the sale of its services and not receive financial assistance from businesses, foundations, or government," as he put it. This board member took great pride in the fact that the trolley company had so far made it on its own and had not "been a drain on foundation monies or public dollars." As he argued, "We never intended the trolley to be on the public dole. It was a public service, but a service which would pay its own way."

Newer board members agreed that the trolley was a public service. However, they argued, having been "enfranchised by government" as a nonprofit organization it was appropriate to obtain government funds, particularly because the Department of Transportation money meant greater safety and the suburban city contract meant more convenient service for tourists to the metropolitan area.

The founding board members prevailed and a decision was made to pursue neither opportunity. However, because of uncertainty about the future of the company and the inability to explore new opportunities for growth, the executive director began to pursue alternative plans for employment and the board president no longer played a major leadership role in moving the board in new directions. The board decided that it would oversee the "best little bus company in town," with a focus on efficient operation and marketing of its existing routes to maximize its income.

What are the general lessons of this example for chief executives? It is important that a board agree about the most fundamental definition of its purpose. We believe that the effective chief executive ensures that the discussion of the mission of the organization is an ongoing process and not a discrete event for the board. Too often mission statements—if they exist at all— are found buried in an organization's files. The statement may come alive once a year at an annual board retreat or dinner, but too often it is not used as a constant reminder of the purpose of the organization, nor is it frequently discussed or revised.

There are three criteria that can help shape agreement about the broadest statement of organizational mission and serve as standards by which to judge clarity of mission and purpose (Bloch, 1988). The first of these is: The mission should reflect a deeply felt sense for the present and desirable future state of the organization; it should make a statement for the present and take a stand for a preferred future for those who have a stake in the organization.

A successful board can learn to define clearly how to measure its success as it moves to capture the future. A well-defined and realistic mission can also serve to stimulate the board to look beyond the goodness of the cause, which is important because it is easy to confuse good intentions with the realities that unstable environments create. A focus upon the uncertain external environment is necessary to understand the real impact of the organization. Moreover, it is from the environment that the resources to run the organization are found.

Success is also measured from outside the organization. While excellent administration can see to it that work is done productively and efficiently, on schedule, and with a high level of quality, it is the satisfaction of stakeholders with the services provided and the willingness of funders to renew resources that are the final measures of success. It is to these measures that a board must constantly attend.

It is common for effective nonprofit boards to set aside time periodically to discuss their mission and future. Such a session can be conducted by a skillful chief executive, the board president, or an outside consultant. We have facilitated many such planning retreats with boards and have found that a good place to begin is with such basic questions as: What is our reason for being? What business are we in?

As Peter Drucker (1974) has said, the answers to these questions are never obvious. One simple technique we have used to help boards discuss purpose and mission is to ask board members to give one-sentence answers to each of these questions. It may be preferable to have these responses written anonymously. As responses are shared, it is not unusual to have significant differences arise.

One of us conducted this experiment with the board of a neighborhood organization. When asked to define the organization's purpose, one board member said matter-of-factly, "Well, that's clear to me, we are here to make sure our home values do not depreciate." Almost immediately there was dissent from another board member who replied, "Hold it! Our concerns are much broader than that. We're here to ensure there is a quality of life which makes it possible for folks who want to live safe and productive lives in our community." "That's too broadly defined," said another. "We can be much more specific. We do rehab work on homes. We provide child care services. We organize block clubs and provide them support."

After lengthy discussion, the group was able to state specifically and clearly its special and concrete program objectives. But it was also able to develop a comprehensive statement of mission that had a unifying effect upon the board. This example brings us to our second criterion for stating an organizational mission: The mission needs to be understood as both strategic and lofty. It is strategic in the sense that it is realistic and credible. It is lofty to the extent that it is an attractive statement that the stakeholders of the organization can understand and embrace (Bloch, 1988).

The mission of the organization can be lofty in the sense that it captures the imagination and engages the spirit; it speaks to something that matters to those who are dedicated to the organization. We believe that it is appropriate for staff, board members, and other volunteers to remind each other about the fundamental values or principles that attracted them to the organization and that sustain their commitment. Individuals serve causes for which they have a passion, and our passions find their taproot in our fundamental values. A reaffirmation of the good intentions of the organization and the causes it serves is not a substitute for results, but it is the kind of reminder that sustains and energizes efforts that can lead to results. It is important for someone to periodically initiate such a discussion of shared values and principles—if it does not originate from the board, the chief executive can do it.

Discussions at this level may in some cases actually be much preferable to specific discussions about goals and objectives. Usually discussions about what will be happening in the next few months are nothing more than conversations about extensions of what has gone on in the past. As a result, an examination of goals and objectives may become too limited and may not be very uplifting. It is our experience that participants sometimes become disheartened during goal-setting meetings. This happens because discussions about goals and objectives reinforce the belief that the future will be no different from the past.

The third criterion for a mission statement is: The mission must be shared by all. By "shared," we mean the mission must be agreed upon by all members of the board; that is, it must be developed jointly. The board should accept input from the chief executive, staff, clients served, and other stakeholders. All should fully understand and accept the mission and direct their efforts toward its achievement.

A shared sense of mission cannot be established by board edict or solely at a planning retreat. It is more an act of ongoing persuasion, a continuing process of consensus building among those involved with the organization. It grows out of a shared sense that the cause is right for the times (funders will support it), right for the organization (those who work on its behalf), and right for the community (those served by the organization, who must also share in its definition).

In the end, it is the leaders of the organization who must articulate the mission and give it legitimacy, who—through this clarification of mission—must engage others to make the decisions to get the right things done. If the mission is to succeed, it must grow out of the needs and interests of the stakeholders of the organization and must be claimed by all the important actors.

To many, these criteria may seem trivial. "Of course we all agree," many board members will say quickly. Seldom, however, does a shared sense of mission develop naturally, nor is it an easy task to define. In most cases, the mission of an organization unfolds slowly and is modified as factors in the environment of the organization change. Board-centered leadership exercised by the chief executive regularly engages the board in thinking about mission and purpose. Such actions can go a long way to ensure that board members not only pull in the same direction but do so with dedication, passion, and purpose.

Board Member Role Expectations

Board membership usually serves many purposes for individual members. The roles assumed by a board member depend on both the expectations of others and on personal desires. In some cases board members may not want to do the things they are asked to do. For volunteers to perform their roles fully, the script must be one with which they feel comfortable.

Consider the case of a substance abuse treatment organization that had always relied on government contracts and grants for all its revenues. With cutbacks and contracts that failed to keep pace with inflation, this organization found itself in a position where other sources of revenue were required. The chief executive saw this necessity coming. She believed it was the board's responsibility to deal with this pending financial difficulty and presented the facts to the board. The board decided to seek private donations, to a total of several thousand dollars. However, neither members of the board nor the executive had any experience with private fund raising.

The board adopted a plan in which each member would raise a specified amount. Soon attendance at board meetings declined precipitously. The board president tried to call members to check on how their efforts were proceeding and to encourage them. Many failed to return calls and some resigned. In short, the board raised very little money and began to distintegrate. By this point, the remaining board members felt the executive had let them down by not taking the lead in fund raising, and she was dismissed.

The board could not find a suitable candidate from outside and soon promoted a program director to chief executive. The new chief executive also lacked fund-raising experience. She did, however, talk with each of the board members privately to ask what they expected of her in the way of fund-raising and other duties, as well as to sound out their views on why the previous fund-raising effort had fallen short and what each member believed he or she could realistically do in fund-raising. The new executive found that the poor fund-raising performance stemmed from the fact that the board members had neither experience nor training in fund raising. She took certain actions to reduce expenses and proposed a smaller fund-raising goal, to be reached through a combination of special events (many board members indicated a greater willingness to work on special events than to ask friends for donations) and board member solicitations. She also worked with the board to develop a plan with which they were more comfortable and provided help in carrying out the plan.

This example illustrates two important lessons about the relations between chief executives and boards. First, as the incumbent executive's handling of the situation shows, it is often *not* sufficient for the executive to assume that a board will meet its obligations, especially when such obligations are newly adopted, unexpected, and unfamiliar. Second, as the next executive's more effective response shows, executives must often help boards meet their responsibilities. By meeting individually with board members, discovering what each wants and feels he or she can do, and developing and following through on plans consistent with these desires, an executive can help a board become more effective.

Board members typically have many reasons for wanting to serve on boards (Widmer, 1989). Some board members are quite flexible and willing to adapt to many different and changing expectations of them. Others may want to perform their roles differently from how others expect them to perform.

Board membership may provide an opportunity to serve a cause. Common interest in a cause can make it possible for board members to work together. These same similarities of interest can be the source of strong social bonds. Friendships can become important sources of attraction for members of a board. Satisfying individual board member interests — which can vary significantly — is what often sustains a board member's active interest in and involvement on a board.

For some, board membership presents an opportunity to become more visible in a community. It is not uncommon for membership on some boards to signify the recognition of an individual's social position. In short, it is much too simple to assume that an interest in the cause of the organization is the only or primary motivation for board service. A board-centered executive is aware that there are multiple motivations board members may have for board service, that board members are, first and foremost, volunteers, and that it is important to know what it is that attracts an individual board member to serve. A framework from social psychology may be helpful in thinking about how this happens.

Thibaut and Kelley (1959) distinguish between the "comparison level" and "comparison level for alternatives" to explain how relationships are sustained. These two concepts describe how individuals select from a possible set of roles and expectations those that are the most attractive. For example, the comparison level is the standard by which an individual evaluates the desirability of membership in a group, and the comparison level alternative is the standard by which individuals compare one group membership to another. Decisions concerning the desirability of membership on a board are made on the basis of the value of one's board membership to its alternatives. The alternative may be service on a different board or in other volunteer activities, or other roles that grant visibility or present opportunities to exercise leadership in a community.

It is fair to recognize that individuals want something from their membership on a board. As they perform their role on the board they get something in return. While most people might prefer a board position where membership provides the maximum number of valued rewards while incurring the fewest number of costs, in most cases "wants" and "gets" are in a fair degree of balance. Indeed, if someone gets little of what he or she wants from board work, he or she will seek balance by reducing the time and effort given to board work.

It is important to remember that these exchanges can occur for both social and task purposes. Individuals join boards because of their desire to get something done that cannot be achieved without other people's help. They also may join boards because of a need to affiliate with others or to meet certain personal psychological needs (for example, to be recognized). Both social relations and the accomplishment of tasks serve as sources of reward.

According to Thibaut and Kelley, we give and get from our interactions with others on the basis of exchanges that meet or do not meet our needs. Our satisfaction in the long run and our sustaining efforts on a board in the short run may depend upon whether we find these exchanges equitable. The skilled board-centered chief executive understands the importance of this equation and how it operates for each board member. Asking in various ways, "What is it you really want from your membership on this board?" and listening carefully to how board members describe what it is they are gaining is a straightforward way to begin to understand how this equation operates. Although some board members are chosen for specific reasons and roles, nothing prevents the executive and board president from making sure a board member understands all the various roles that are needed on a board. For example, creating opportunities for long-standing board members to do or to learn new things is a good tactic to help keep them vital and involved. Investing time with a new board to outline the various ways board roles can be fulfilled can have significant long-term payoff.

Over time, some boards tend to evolve into highly interdependent systems with relatively stable relationships in which the exchange in "wants" and "gets" is regularly satisfied. Such boards are usually able to establish effective cooperative efforts among members. On other boards, competition and dissatisfaction among members can unfortunately be the rule, and unresolved conflicts of interest and unfulfilled expectations can destabilize the board and make its work difficult. It is important to recognize that it is part of the effective chief executive's responsibility to ensure that the exchange process for individual board members is experienced as fair and subject to renegotiation. The skilled executive works very closely with the board president in carrying out this responsibility.

Competitiveness on boards, when it exists, usually occurs when members see themselves as competing for mutually exclusive goals rather than working for a shared or common interest. Role dissatisfactions occur when individuals do not receive a sense of reward for the investments they make in the organization. Significantly greater productivity can be expected from boards comprised of individuals who share fully in an agreed-upon mission of the organization and for whom the exchanges are experienced as equitable.

Central to the resolution of differences on a board is the discovery of a common purpose. The issue of cooperation versus conflict on a board and the importance of relationships defined as exchanges help us understand ways to think about how to bring a board together. If boards become too absorbed in the task (the cause), they may neglect the social needs of members for whom simply belonging to a board provides much satisfaction. If boards pay too much attention to the satisfaction of individual needs and fulfillment of personal role expectations, a sense of shared purpose may be lost. Tension in the relationships among individual board members is resolved around the interplay of different "wants" and "gets" and the sense of common purpose. As boards resolve differences, satisfy individual member needs, and devise ways to establish cooperative relations, they evolve in one way. When these issues are not resolved they evolve in another way. Some boards compete; some cooperate. Some stagnate; others are vibrant and alive. Some just disintegrate. We know of no other way for boards to find a balance between individual "wants" and "gets" than to talk openly about these needs. The effective chief executive knows how to engage in and encourage such communications.

Dealing with Factions

Because of the failure of some boards to arrive at a shared purpose and a satisfactory exchange of "wants" and "gets," boards can develop factions that in some cases develop intractable differences. Boards, like every other human group, develop sub-groups or cliques that may be the source of major differences. Such sub-groups typically are based on prior friendships and demographic similarities (such as occupation, life cycle stage, and so on). However, these kinds of cliques are usually unrelated to differing positions on organizational issues. Factions occur when sub-groups develop over sharp and continuing differences on matters of organizational mission.

For instance, when the board of an organization that provided services to developmentally disabled adults added new members, some with professional training and others without such training, a split developed over whether the organization's mission and programs should provide maximum independence or protection for clients. The professional faction favored maximum independence, which meant a greater emphasis on life skills, work training, and eventual movement, if appropriate, from group homes to apartment living. The other faction favored protection, with an emphasis on fun (including substantial preparation for Special Olympics events) and on maintaining the family feeling of group homes. The professional faction talked of "clients" and "individual habilitation plans," while the other faction talked of "taking care of the kids." These differing conceptions soon came to affect much of the board's decision making as each faction sought to advance its agenda in whatever way possible.

Not surprisingly, the chief executive and senior staff shared the views of the professional faction, and the organization had increasingly been managed to achieve maximum independence of clients. Eventually the protectionist faction called for a showdown on a vote for funding a new summer recreation program. Several members stated that if the program was not approved they would resign. Ultimately the decision rested with a few members who were not a part of either faction and who had participated least in board activities. These individuals voted almost fully with the professional faction (whether because they wanted to be rid of discord, because they were convinced that the professional faction was right, or because they disliked the tactics of the protectionists is not known), and most of the protectionists resigned.

Factionalized boards, though exceedingly uncomfortable for all concerned, cannot and probably should not always be considered a problem. The uses and advantages of organizational conflict, if successfully resolved, have become much more widely recognized (Robbins, 1974). The most fundamental advantage of conflict is that it signals an opportunity, perhaps a need, for change. As the foregoing example shows, the factionalization on the board was related to the fundamental mission and goals of the organization. Thus, it was necessary that this conflict surface and be resolved. Perhaps the conflict could have been more skillfully and quickly handled. However, the important lesson is that, in spite of the stress and discomfort conflict usually brings, conflict must be accepted and built on. An organization is a coalition of stakeholders with varying interests, among whom agreements have been reached about what each stakeholder will contribute and receive. However, the stability of these agreements is likely to be only temporary as new stakeholders present their expectations or old stakeholders change their expectations or reassess the equity of the agreement. Thus, the potential for disagreement over what the organization does, for whom, and how, is substantial. In fact, the disagreements or conflicts that get expressed are probably only a small fraction of the potential or latent conflicts that could be expressed. Those disagreements that do surface represent an opportunity for a change in the terms of the coalition agreement or in the coalition itself.

Not all stakeholder parties to the organizational coalition will have the same interest in or commitment to the continuing existence of the specific organization. Funders, accrediting bodies, and governmental regulators, for example, may care very little whether a specific nonprofit service provider continues to exist. Clients and their relatives, on the other hand, may have a significant attachment to a particular organization, and long-time donors, past and current board members, and especially staff may have the greatest interest in the continuance of a particular organization. Such differences will usually mean that those with the greatest interest or commitment to a specific organization will respond to conflict about organizational purposes or processes in ways that are likely to maintain the existence of the organization. That is, it is *individuals,* who may be agents or representatives of other constituencies as well, with interests in the continuance of a specific organization who respond to conflict by using it to institute changes that position the organization for continued success. Self-perpetuating nonprofit boards are probably less likely to be conflictive than boards elected by a membership. In either case, board members are likely to have or to develop a commitment to organizational survival. Such a commitment does not mean disagreements will not arise, but it does ensure a certain measure of commonality. Common commitment to organizational continuance probably accounts, in part, for the rarity of factionalized boards.

Discussing Role Expectations and Board Performance with the Board

What can a chief executive do to initiate discussions about role expectations and board performance? The effective chief executive engages in regular face-to-face meetings with most of the board members and most regularly with the board president. During these discussions it is crucial that the executive sound out how board members feel about the board's performance and their roles on it. While the discussion might begin with a review of some current organizational issue, the executive will want to direct the conversation toward board performance. If problems in board performance are uncovered, the executive will want to engage in a supportive, problem-solving communication style, stating how she or he feels, treating the problem as "our" not "your" or "their" problem, and inviting the board member to react.

These discussions are important opportunities for the executive to gain feedback from board members about anything in the relationship between board members and the chief executive that is troubling. In addition to learning how the president and other board members feel about the board's performance and the chief executive's role, a key purpose of these meetings can be to find a champion of change. It is obviously desirable that the board president become the major advocate for improving the way the board performs. If that turns out not to be the case, at least initially, it is nonetheless crucial that the executive find, encourage, and work with a champion. It is virtually impossible for an executive to reenergize a board on which no one recognizes the need for and is willing to work toward making improvements. We believe that on nearly every board there are some, often many, who are willing to do more. Usually they need the support and encouragement of others, especially an attentive chief executive.

In addition to finding a champion, the executive will also find, in most cases, some other members supportive of change. As the one-on-one meetings proceed, the executive will probably learn what changes in his or her relationships with board members are desired and can begin to implement these. The executive will also want to see that the champion and his or her supporters take an active, up-front position in initiating changes in procedures and expectations. That is, the champion's group, rather than the executive, should propose changes to others on the board. The executive's role is to provide information, suggestions, and encouragement to this group.

Board Recruitment

Too often, likely causes of inadequate board performance are poor recruitment, orientation, and training of new members. The role played here by the chief executive can often be critical. Ideally, board selection calls for a systematic assessment of board strengths and weaknesses through the use of a profile grid, and then a search for candidates who will remove the weaknesses. In reality, the process followed may be much less systematic. Members may nominate, and ultimately select, friends and associates. Similarly, the ideal approach envisions a thorough interview of candidates in which they receive accurate information about the organization's goals, programs, and finances, and about what will be expected of them in terms of time, effort, and fund raising (including personal giving). Candidates may be asked to explain why they are interested in serving on the board. Our impression is that this careful interviewing process occurs very infrequently.

Thus, a common board reality is that many new members join with unclarified or minimal expectations. Boards have great difficulty breaking this cycle on their own. The chief executive will likely have occasion to intervene in this cycle and suggest certain substantive changes in the recruitment, orientation, and expectations of the board. One recommended practice (for example, O'Connell, 1985; Houle, 1989) is the adoption of a nominating committee. This committee's job is to assess what skills and personal characteristics are needed on the board, determine the extent to which the current board meets those needs, and develop and follow through on procedures for identifying, recruiting, and selecting future board members. (Boards that are not self-perpetuating will have to adapt their procedures to fit their circumstances.)

The nominating committee may also want to reexamine standards of board performance, including policies regarding attendance at board or committee meetings, handling of expected donations, and management of board rotation. Finally, this committee should actively identify individuals for upcoming board vacancies and undertake initial interviews with possible candidates in which the candidates receive realistic information about work on the board and the organization's mission, programs, and financial position.

The executive's role in relation to the nominating committee is that of staff consultant or adviser. The executive may want to suggest the names of potential candidates, after making sure that doing so is acceptable to the board president and the chairperson of the nominating committee. While the executive may help draft the letter requesting an interview, she or he should avoid conducting interviews. Usually, only a board member (or members) should be present at such interviews.

Orientation of New Board Members

The orientation of new members, of course, begins when they are first approached about becoming a candidate. The official orientation occurs after a new member has been selected. Soon after selection, a visit to the organization's offices and facilities should be scheduled. Ideally, the tour is led by an experienced board member, with the executive accompanying. The point of the tour is to provide an overview of the organization in operation, to allow the new member to meet some of the staff, and to begin to provide detailed information about the organization and the work of the board. Sometimes it's helpful to have two or three new members on the same tour. Doing so is more efficient and also begins to introduce members to each other and build a team. The end of the tour is an appropriate time for the new members to receive any necessary written materials.

Houle (1989) has provided a useful list of the documents that should constitute the board manual. They include: the constitution or articles of incorporation; the bylaws; a description of the organization's programs; an annual schedule or plan of work for the board; a board roster; a list of committees, with a statement of the purposes and duties of each; a statement of board policies; an organization chart; and a current budget. At some point new members should also receive copies of the board minutes for the previous year.

A technique that we think especially useful is to provide new members with a mentor or buddy, an experienced member who checks periodically with the new member to see if he or she has the necessary information and encourages the new member to call with questions. Of course, the chief executive should also encourage new members to call him or her.

The first board meeting that newly selected members will attend needs to feature not only name introductions but an occasion for more thorough introductions. Such introductions might call for each member (new and continuing) to tell about his or her background, why they serve on this board, and what each especially contributes, or expects to contribute, to the work of this board.

The process of initiating the sorts of changes we have advocated in this chapter in a lackluster board is usually incremental. Such changes cannot be accomplished in a week or two. The process may take months and will have the greatest effect when new members are added. Sometimes the executive may feel that an outside consultant could help advance the process. Certainly a consultant can provide legitimacy to a change effort. Many consultants are skilled in helping board members accept and identify problems and in facilitating group processes for finding and implementing solutions. In many cities there are nonprofit consulting agencies that work exclusively with other nonprofit organizations. Most United Ways also provide such consulting services to their affiliates. Both typically operate on a sliding-scale basis or otherwise provide relatively inexpensive consultation.

The advantage of using a skilled consultant is that doing so somewhat depersonalizes and speeds up the process. However, we believe changes in board functioning can be initiated and achieved without the assistance of consultants. If board members desire authoritative statements about the roles, responsibilities, and processes of nonprofit boards, the National Center for Nonprofit Boards (2000 L Street, N.W., Suite 411, Washington, DC 20036; 202 452-6262) has a wide variety of materials available, many of which are especially designed for board members.

SIX

Learning Board-Centered Leadership Skills: Guidelines for the Chief Executive

oooooooooooooooooooooooooooooooooooooooooooooooo

The research upon which this book is based began with a series of questions. What are the special skills and abilities that distinguish the work of the most successful nonprofit leaders? Can these characteristics be identified and assessed? If these questions could be adequately answered, we believed we could contribute to a growing body of research about leadership in nonprofit organizations. We also wished to be better prepared to assist those interested in learning about the specific actions that result in effective nonprofit organizational leadership.

The Theory and Practice of Successful Executive Leadership

We have confidence that our research has been successful in advancing a more thorough understanding of the nature of leadership and management in nonprofit organizations. We also believe our findings contribute to the development of a more systematic and empirically based theory of nonprofit leadership. It is now possible for us to talk about the qualities and characteristics of effective leadership with a reasonable degree of assurance. We have decidedly clearer ideas about the actions associated with effective nonprofit organizational leadership, which we define as board-centered leadership by the chief executive.

The purpose of this chapter is to provide clearer prescriptions for the improved practice of board-centered leadership. We will further describe the six specific sets of behaviors that we found characterized successful chief executives. We also offer ways for the reader to consider how one goes about learning these behaviors.

Before undertaking our research we were able to make only indirect and often tenuous inferences about successful nonprofit leadership. At a most general level we can now conclude (managed systems theory to the contrary) that chief executives, not the board, are centrally responsible for success and failure in nonprofit organizations. This is not to suggest, however, a diminished role for the board. We also conclude that effective nonprofit executive leadership is characterized by activities directed externally with and through the board. Attention must be directed specifically at the management of problems having to do with resource acquisition.

Our model of effective nonprofit leadership and its standards for board-centered executive leadership derive from the practice of successful chief executives. However, adapting the model to one's own circumstances is not likely to be easy. It is one thing to become aware of the characteristics of effective leadership—for example, the importance of what we call creative boundary spanning. It is quite another matter to translate that knowledge into skillful behavior.

We are accustomed, just as are our students, to expect that a good part of management education is necessarily characterized by a significant measure of "aboutism." We talk a lot about things with our students. For example, an aspiring nonprofit executive would most certainly want to know about the central role of the voluntary sector in contemporary society. It would also be helpful to know something about the contributing social theories that help explain the prevailing patterns of voluntary action in the United States. Elegantly developed theories about the third sector provide important grounding for an informed student of the nonprofit sector.

Too frequently, however, such descriptions fall far short of providing insights into the competencies necessary to deal effectively with the circumstances we do such a fine job describing. We hope the exposition of the preceding five chapters as it weaves back and forth between data and theory, between cases and theoretical concepts, and between description and prescription does so in such a way as to assist the reader in gaining insight into the connection between knowledge and skill, research and practice. In short, we believe in the value of our research to improve practical skills.

Learning To Be More Skillful

Clearly, effective leadership in nonprofit organizations is to be found in actions taken to develop an effective board. The chief executive usually plays a central role in such actions; nonprofit organizations and boards do not become effective just by happenstance. However, effective leadership rarely just occurs. One way or another, successful chief executives must learn to behave in effective, board-centered ways.

We are hardly the first to have wrestled with the complexities of trying to explain to others how to behave more competently. In fact, there is a longstanding appreciation of this problem in the management literature. Many scholars of management share a similar set of assumptions pertinent to this issue. The first assumption argues that the learning of skills and the learning of knowledge are not incompatible; that is, one does not negate the other. The second assumption addresses how this kind of learning can occur. Skill learning requires knowledge plus insights from practice plus feedback. For example, Argyris and Schön (1975) argue that it is critical for managers to distinguish between the theories they espouse (what they think they do) and the theories they use (what they actually do). They suggest that managers need feedback about their practices in order to gain insight into the incongruities between these two kinds of theory.

A similar point was made in the management literature over forty years ago in an eloquent argument by Fritz J. Roethelisberger. This pioneering researcher (one of those involved in the classic Hawthorn studies) discussed the problems and challenges in applying what we know to the solution of problems in organizations.

So the conclusion I find myself reaching more and more is that our practical solutions of applying what we know to organizations depend upon introducing into the social system a self-aware person with skills of an unusually high order. Not only does [the manager] need skills of diagnosis; [the manager] also needs skills of communication, i.e., skills of securing understanding of people. Above all, [the manager] has to be aware of himself and the effect of his behavior on others.

It is not enough that [the manager] has a capacity to assess the personal and social determinants in a concrete piece of behavior, which is what I mean by diagnostic skill. This kind of understanding gives insight only to the practitioner of the skill. In human situations [the practitioner's] understanding is not enough; rather the persons in the situation must have it. To develop such understanding requires another kind of skill. It is a skill which helps others secure understanding of the problems that affect them. In many human situations this is the kind of skill needed. Without it all our diagnostic skills become ineffectual or obsessively elaborated. We are trying to solve the problem from the "outside"; we are trying to superimpose our understanding on the understanding of others. As a result we provoke anxiety, apprehension, resistance, and feelings of dependence upon the expert.

Although these two skills, capacity to understand situations and capacity to help others develop understanding, are closely related, they are not the same. Experience has repeatedly shown that a person who is skilled in the first does not necessarily have skills in communicating his understanding to those who need it [Roethelisberger, 1968, p. 113].

Both these points of view — the notion of "espoused theories" versus "theories in use" as developed by Argyris and Schön, and the insights of self-awareness and the skills of helping others elaborated by Roethelisberger — are starting points for understanding how one begins to learn more about effective practice. In brief, these authors argue that learning begins with the capacity to understand one's relationhip to the situation, with a *balanced* awareness of one's self and the impact one's actions have upon the situation and the other individuals involved. For Argyris and Schön this self-awareness diminishes the discrepancies between espoused theories and theories in use. For Roethelisberger, the development of this kind of self-awareness is central to the skills of diagnosis, the skills of action, and the skills of helping.

How Successful Executives
Learn To Be Board-Centered

Evidence from some additional research we've done suggests that successful chief executives, those who are more inclined to work with and through their boards, are more likely to turn to their boards to learn board-centered skills. In short, successful chief executives are more inclined to deal directly with their boards in learning to be more effective. Once our research established the importance of board-centered skills, we were curious whether the executives in our study could tell us anything about how these skills are learned. In a follow-up study of the especially effective and comparison executives we asked both groups, "From whom did you learn the most useful things about working with boards after you became a chief executive?"

The effective executives more frequently responded that they learned from their board president and/or other board members (Herman and Heimovics, 1989). No doubt other factors are important in accounting for acquiring board-centered skills, but a willingness to learn directly from the board in the here and now of everyday work is apparently an important place to begin. We believe this evidence is affirmation of the ideas of how we learn to become more skillful as argued by Roethelisberger and by Argyris and Schon. Apparently, successful chief executives find ways to be open with their boards to learn how they can be more board-centered.

Curiously, more than half of our effective chief executives in the follow-up study indicated that they had no prior experience working with boards, whereas all of the comparison executives had some prior work experience with boards. This surprising finding suggests that experience working with a board is no guarantee of, nor even a prerequisite to, effective board-centered leadership. Rather, it seems most likely that effective chief executives have learned something about how to reconcile their espoused theories and theories in use and have determined how to work openly and directly with their boards to address issues of relationship building and role clarification.

The Board-Centered Chief Executive

The six crucial leadership skills identified and discussed below can provide the starting place for a chief executive and board to understand and address the role, relationships, and responsibilities of the board-centered chief executive. The effective manifestation of these behaviors by the chief executive can lead, we believe, to four important outcomes: a board that understands and is committed to its mission, a board on which members work cooperatively toward common goals, a board on which members' needs and interests are addressed and generally satisfied, and a board that engages in the requisite policy-making roles and willingly responds to the challenge of resource acquisition and development.

In both the classroom and in our consulting work, we have experimented with a variety of ways to help chief executives and board members think and learn about being more board-centered. A first step is for the executive to become an expert diagnostician of the board. As we have argued earlier, and as Roethelisberger suggests, the skills of effective board-centered leadership are most likely found in those executives who have finely honed their ability to understand the work of the board as a whole in all its complexity. This means recognizing the needs and interdependencies of various board members, understanding how the actions of certain board members add to or detract from the overall effectiveness of the board, and understanding how goals are set and the role individual board members play in setting those goals.

We noted that board work is an ongoing process and not a discrete event and that the causes of problems unfold over time. Therefore it is helpful for the executive to view the board as an ongoing system of social interaction. From this perspective, patterns of relationships and communication are developed among board members and between a board and its executive director. It is in the context of these ongoing interactions that the successful chief executive engages in board-centered behaviors.

It is common for effective nonprofit boards to periodically set aside time to discuss how their work is proceeding and to examine their way of doing business, their mission, and their future. Such a session can be conducted by a skillful board president, the chief executive, or an outside consultant. We have facilitated many such sessions with boards and have found that they can lead to a clearer sense of organizational direction and priorities. It is less common for a board and chief executive to address directly the ways that the chief executive can work more effectively with the board. We believe that this kind of openness is a key to successful leadership in nonprofit organizations.

The Six Requisite Skills of the
Board-Centered Chief Executive

What then are the six specific sets of behaviors that characterize the work of successful chief executives? Our research identifies them as:

1. Facilitating interaction in board relationships.
2. Showing consideration and respect toward board members.
3. Envisioning change and innovation with the board.
4. Promoting board accomplishments and productivity.
5. Initiating and maintaining a structure for board work.
6. Providing helpful information to the board.

In the balance of this chapter we will examine each of these six sets of behaviors. We identify a number of questions that a practicing chief executive and board members can ask to assess the extent to which the chief executive engages in board-centered leadership. A comparison of the answers can contribute to a better congruence between a chief executive's espoused theory of leadership and an effective theory of action.

Facilitating Interaction in Board Relationships. Does the chief executive encourage and solicit full participation by all board members? Is the executive skillful in helping the board achieve consensus about important matters? Is the executive helpful in resolving differences among members of the board? Does the executive view the board as a team where individual member's contributions are prized and where collective efforts are encouraged and valued as much as those of individual members?

The successful chief executive pays attention to and works to see that board members engage in satisfying and productive interaction with each other and with the executive. In short, board meetings and other aspects of board work are experienced as gratifying and constructive because board members individually and collectively believe they have contributed in meaningful ways to each other and to the work of the organization.

The executive helps the board seek consensus. It is important to remember that unanimity and consensus are not the same thing. The goal of consensus is to ensure that all points of view on a board are heard, all positions are understood and carefully considered. Differences of opinion are to be expected and are considered natural parts of the decision-making process. Disagreements are viewed as positive ways to open decisions of the board to wider ranges of information, opinions, and options.

Formal board meetings are not always the best place to pound out a consensus on a tough decision. Board meetings are to be considered singularly important and among the few times when the full board and key staff come together. Although there will always be differences of opinion expressed at board meetings, major conflicts are best resolved by the appropriate parties prior to formal meetings of the board. Board meetings are valuable times to discuss issues and to decide courses of action.

However, the board meeting is not the best time for sides to be taken, negotiations to be made, or compromises to be reached.

The skillful chief executive is close enough to the positions, concerns, and interests of each board member to not be caught off guard if a board member objects strongly to an idea from another board member. In these circumstances, the effective executive can ensure that differences are heard and understood. But whenever possible differences among board members should be satisfactorily worked through prior to the issue being taken before the full board. It is important that board meetings run smoothly and efficiently. Board members should leave a meeting with a sense of direction and a feeling of accomplishment and closure on important issues, not with feelings of frustration or anger associated with unresolved conflict.

A helpful technique is for the executive to assist board members to "separate the problem from the people" (Fisher and Ury, 1983 p. 17). Serving as a facilitative third party at meetings with conflicting parties, keeping careful tabs on attendance of committees, ensuring that missing members are brought up to date, and working carefully with the board president to ensure that all parties are fundamentally in agreement before any important actions are taken are all strategies to ensure that board members are hard on the problem but not on each other.

Showing Consideration and Respect Toward Board Members. Is the executive sensitive to board members' interests and wants? Does the executive show concern for board members' needs? Is the executive fair and objective with all board members?

In order for a chief executive to help a board engage in constructive interaction, he or she should be skilled at listening to board members and should be able to hear the concerns that reside behind their words. In Chapter Five we discussed the importance of the executive listening to what board members want from membership on a board. It is equally important for the executive to become aware of what a board member is getting in return. Board membership is an exchange. While some individuals might prefer a board position that provides the maximum number of valued rewards for the least possible cost, in most cases "wants" and "gets" should be in a fair degree of balance. In fact, as volunteers, it is safe to assume that most board members are willing to give a lot. However, it should also be noted that if a board member gets little of what he or she wants from membership on the board, that member may seek a balance by reducing the time and effort given to board work.

In our own work with boards we find it helpful (and so might the skillful chief executive) to ask board members to be clear with themselves and open with each other about why they are on the board and what it is they want from their board membership. A simple exercise of listing "wants" and sharing "gets" — both those desired and those not desired — can be an effective way for board members to be clear with each other and with the chief executive about what matters to them in their board membership. It is the chance for members to share the fundamental reasons they wish to serve the organization. It is important to encourage and recognize in such experiments that it is legitimate for individuals to express "wants" that may be much more than simply serving a particular cause.

In summary, the successful executive is aware of the needs of each board member (face-to-face meetings with individual board members are especially useful in this regard) and responds to those needs. While members typically have mulitple motives for joining boards (Widmer, 1989), one or two are usually of greater importance. For instance, some members may seek sociability from memberships. The executive can suggest to the board president that they be placed on committees with others they like or develop group projects on which they can work. Other members may want to develop certain skills, and the executive can find ways to make this happen. In short, the executive recognizes and respects that the board member's relation to the organization is fundamentally one of exchange. For their contribution, board members expect something in return: friendship, skill development, useful personal contacts, recognition, feelings of accomplishment, and so on.

Envisioning Change and Innovation for the Organization in Work with the Board. Does the executive play a central role in sensing the changing external environment and developing strategic responses to changes in the environment? Does the executive engage the board in seeking new and better ways to deal with old problems? Does the executive originate efforts to explore new funding opportunities? Does the executive regularly ask the board to discuss its mission, and is the executive helpful to a board in redefining its mission in response to changes in the environment? Is the executive tolerant of ambiguity and helpful to the board in taking informed risks?

Chapter Four describes the work of the executive across the boundaries of the organization. Nonprofit organizations are characterized as open systems with permeable boundaries affected significantly by factors in the environment. A crucial leadership role for the chief executive is to continually attend to the relationship of the organization to a changing environment. Executives must keep board members apprised of the trends, changing circumstances, and unexpected occurrences that could call for adaptation or innovation. The executive will want to lay a trail that leads toward major decisions. The executive will encourage the board to consider new opportunities and to look for better ways of doing things and better things to do.

Chapter Five describes in some detail the importance of clarifying the mission of the organization. It is highly unlikely for chief executives to act independently as attempts are made to position their organization in the environment. These activities will ultimately engage the board. So too must the board, with the executive's help, regularly review and discuss its mission statement.

Initiating and Maintaining Structure for the Board. Does the executive ensure that board members are adequately prepared for meetings with advanced agendas, materials, and information? Are helpful minutes or records kept, collected in such ways as to record decisions and critical discussions? Are the assignments and individual responsibilities of board members clear? Do individual board members know what is expected of them by the chief executive, by the board president, and by fellow board members? Are meetings well run? Are goals clear, and are members really sure of what it is they are trying to accomplish, and can they make judgments about when they have accomplished their goals?

Like all work groups, boards require the materials, schedules, and work plans necessary to achieve their objectives. Effective executives take responsibility to work with the board president and other members to develop and maintain consistent procedures. For instance, establishing an agreed-upon schedule of board and committee meetings for the coming year, seeing that the agenda and other materials are distributed well in advance of meetings, and defining the objectives of each committee transform the somewhat abstract board responsibilities into manageable parts. It is important that the board develop and maintain a routine. It is also important that the board, with advice and encouragement from the chief executive, establish annual objectives. Particular objectives, of course, will vary with the circumstances of each organization. One board may decide to seek a 10 percent increase in contributions. Another may decide to seek accreditation. Whatever objectives are selected, a work plan, schedule, and task assignments must also be established and accepted. The executive will want to monitor the progress of the work toward objectives and provide feedback (or see that it is provided) on progress.

We have found it helpful for the agenda of board meetings to be organized around three separate kinds of items: information to share, issues to discuss, and actions to take. Information to share includes all the relevant and important data the board should know about. Background budget data, information about key meetings and deadlines, updates on programs and proposals, progress reports on the accomplishment of goals, and all the other kinds of important information should be made regularly available to all board members on a need-to-know basis. Although some information is obviously best shared in written form, it should be expected that some board members will be more apt to read written reports than others. Time can be set aside to clarify information at board meetings, but board members can be encouraged not to waste board meeting time when an answer to a clarifying question can be gotten from a secretary or a staff member.

Central to building a board meeting agenda is the ability to know when it is time to bring an action item before a board for a decision. Issues to discuss are *not* actions to take, and the distinction is a critical one. Some issues, particularly important ones that may bear upon the organization's mission or resource base, need ongoing discussion by board members. Some issues may never move off a discussion agenda to action status. Decisions that are ready for action are those that have already been discussed thoroughly by the board. At this point, all major differences have been resolved, all relevant input has been sought, and ideally there will be few surprises for anyone about the outcome. On effective boards, members understand and adhere to (and chief executives help create) the norm that differences between board members will have been resolved before the board meets.

Typically, a board meeting is conducted by the board president. Ideally, the president is able to keep discussions on target, can monitor and direct meetings to keep things moving, and can engage the board in those activities that are stimulating and motivating to members. If in the judgment of the chief executive a board president is unskillful or unfamiliar with the competencies necessary to run good meetings, the executive is faced with a choice of either finding ways to help the president improve meeting skills, working with the president to share the responsibility of running meetings, or accepting the risk that meetings will be unproductive. In any case, the executive who is skillful outside the board meetings in consensus building, in framing action agendas for committees, and in sharing information can go a long way to make meetings much more productive.

Promoting Board Accomplishments and Productivity. Is the chief executive sufficiently concerned with the efficient use of board members' time and efforts? Are there ways for a board to assess the extent to which it is engaged in productive work? Has the executive helped develop standards for the board to use to determine if it is meeting deadlines? Does someone, such as the board president or chief executive, follow-through with board members to see that assignments they have accepted are being completed?

The effective chief executive works to see that the board is a productive one. Actions are taken and successes noted. Infrequently does an effective board come up with specific items that do not result in some kind of action.

Since the skillful executive has listened carefully and knows what is on the mind of all board members and has taken steps to address individual concerns, there are few axes to grind or hidden agendas when the board comes together. Meetings do not evolve into discussions or arguments that only one or two think are important because there is general agreement about what needs to be done. To the extent possible, meetings can include celebration of agreements already made or conflicts previously resolved.

The executive helps to set and maintain high standards, not just for the output of the organization, but for what it means to be a contributing board member. The executive, through the board president and committee chairs, encourages board members to complete tasks and meet deadlines. Board members should also feel they are given recognition for their efforts.

Committee work is used and valued. The successful executive works to ensure that committee work actually does make a contribution to the organization. Some board decision-making authority is delegated to committees. However, committees often operate out of touch with other parts of the board, and it is the executive's job to ensure that the committee is kept on track and aware of where its recommendations may be in conflict with or overlap the work of other committees.

Providing Useful and Helpful Information to the Board. Does the executive collect and distribute information to the board and differentiate between information that may affect the organization and information that does not? Is the information succinctly and clearly presented? Does the executive seek to facilitate shared understanding among board members and use, when they are available, multiple channels of communication? Does the executive have a good sense of where various projects stand and communicate this to the board?

Because the chief executive will often be at the center of

information flow and have access to a great deal of information of all kinds and quality, an effective board depends on the executive for important, decision-relevant, timely information. Obviously, boards require certain routine information, such as financial statements, budget reports, and program service data. As Bader (1989) has demonstrated, such reports can be presented either in ways that are difficult to understand and not especially useful for decision making or in ways that are understandable to all and conducive to decision making. For example, reports that give figures for only one month, quarter, or year are not very useful. Rather, it is desirable to show trends and comparisons. For example, one might want to look at the movement in unit costs or revenues over several periods. Or one might want to contrast figures for this month or quarter with the same period a year ago, or contrast the organization's figures with the industry or field average, if such data are available.

In addition to the typical financial and program data, which tell something of what happened in the past, boards also need information about the present and the future. This sort of information is of a more ambiguous character. It is perhaps better described as inferences based on various clues. Such inferences must often be tentative. For example, a chief executive might strike up a conversation with a foundation official at some meeting and learn that the foundation is considering a proposal from a certain nonprofit organization whose type of services the foundation has never previously funded. This piece of information might have several implications, some of which could be important to the chief executive's organization. Other clues, picked up in other places from other sources, might reinforce or clarify the earlier information. As the meaning of the various clues became clearer, the chief executive would want to share his or her impressions and possible conclusions with at least some members of the board.

We earlier stressed the importance of one-on-one meetings with board members for reviving a poorly performing board. Such face-to-face meetings are also important to maintain an effective board. Generally, an executive will want to have at least one such meeting with every board member annually, and more often if possible. An executive will probably want much more frequent meetings with the board president, chair of the nominating committee, and other key members. The purposes of such meetings are to share the soft, ambiguous clues (including those board members pick up), think about what they might mean for the organization, and, by doing so, build trust.

One of the key rules followed by effective executives is: *no surprises*. Chief executives and the organization they lead most often get into trouble when the executive hides or delays providing bad news. Being the bearer of bad news is, of course, uncomfortable, at best. We're all well aware that messengers are blamed for the message. Such a practice is likely to be especially pronounced when the messenger is the executive who, as we've maintained, is treated by others and by him- or herself as centrally responsible for success and failure.

The understandable temptation to hide bad news, usually with the hope that the problem can be fixed, sometimes leads to an escalation of the seriousness of the problem. Consider the case of an executive who was informed that a change in state procedures meant that certain client expenses would no longer be reimbursed. The executive believed that this was unfair and that he could successfully reverse this state action. While pursuing that course of action, the organization's cash flow deteriorated and the executive used money reserved to meet unemployment payments to cover current bills. He did not succeed in reversing the state action and eventually had to go to the board to ask for an emergency fund-raising effort. When the board found out what had happened, they decided to cut two staff positions and use their salaries to meet obligations. This executive's behavior clearly seems stupid, but there are apparently many similar incidents. Effective executives realize that problems are inevitable and learn to pass along the bad news when the problem is still small. By doing so, executives not only avoid escalating a small problem into a larger one but also are in a position to get help from the board in finding a solution.

Another practice many effective executives use is that of providing periodic written reports to the board. Usually these go out with other reports and agenda prior to monthly board meetings. The format and style of such reports vary, but they often include summaries of the past month's activities, updates on projects in progress, and discussion of emerging and continuing issues. Such reports help to focus the board on the nonroutine and offer another opportunity for the executive to lay a bread crumb trail toward future outcomes.

The six board leadership skills described above provide the tools for developing and maintaining an active, effective board. Executives who consistently exercise these skills will have boards that understand and are committed to the mission, accept and work with the executive in carrying out the policy-making role, and willingly respond to the challenge of resource development. As we argued here and in Chapters Four and Five, an active, effective board gives nonprofit organizations and their chief executives a decisive edge in managing environmentally contingent resource acquisition. Or, to put it another way, executive board leadership skills create boards that are more willing and able to respond to the constantly changing environments of nonprofit organizations.

AFTERWORD

The Chief Executive's Responsibility for Organizational Success

oooooooooooooooooooooooooooooooooooooooooooooooo

Nonprofit chief executives are centrally responsible for the success and failure of their organization. The unique position they hold is based on a leadership of responsibility rather than a leadership of formal authority. This central leadership position does not square with the traditional managed systems model, which places ultimate authority and responsibility with the board. Especially effective chief executives have discovered how to deal with this paradox. They have created and enact an alternative model. They accept their central leadership responsibility, yet work to ensure that their boards fulfill their organizational and public roles. Successful executives engage in board-centered leadership, taking responsibility, as necessary, for initiating and facilitating the work of their boards. Successful chief executives enable boards to work the way they are supposed to work.

In short, our study of successful chief executives found them providing significantly more leadership for their boards than those not deemed especially successful. Furthermore, they work with and through their boards to position their organization in its environment. Effort is directed externally across the boundaries of the organization to manage the organization's dependence on those external factors that determine the availability of the resources necessary to carry out its mission. Boundary-

128

spanning executives also seek opportunities in the environment to help shape the future health and direction of the organization.

Why do some executives engage in more external and board-centered actions than other executives? What sort of transformation has taken place that results in a different way of thinking about the place of the organization in its environment, the role of the board in the organization, and the role of the chief executive in relationship to the board? Why is it that some executives are more able to see their organizations as part of a greater whole and more effective at initiating action?

We cannot answer these questions with much certainty. While they are important questions, the more important reality is that successful chief executives have learned to do so. So can others. The last three chapters of this book offer insights about how successful chief executives use board-centered leadership skills. These skills provide a basis for our specific advice to chief executives who want to know how to span the boundaries of their organizations and work more effectively with their boards.

When we describe the board-centered leadership model and allied skills to our students and to practitioners, we find that some understand these insights quickly and easily. We are given good examples of how they might behave in this way. Others to whom we have described our views may understand the ideas but are less skillful in making the translation from knowledge about to practice of the kind of successful executive leadership we define. Why is there this difference in the ability to think and act in this way? We offer only speculative answers.

The traditional view of nonprofit organizations with the board at the top is a reflection of much of contemporary management theory and practice. This theory is based upon a hierarchical logic and certain assumptions about rational action. Some theorists see the world as much more orderly and rational than do others. So too do some executives.

However, the reality of nonprofit organizational life is that it is much more dynamic than the traditional, hierarchical model can ever grasp. That phrase "strange loops and tangled hierarchies" is much more illustrative of the way the board-executive relationship works than are the formal arrangements implied by the traditional hierarchical perspective. The reality is that leadership in nonprofit organizations does not follow the rules or prescriptions that flow from the traditional, managed systems model. Leadership derives from a much more dynamic pattern of expectations and behavioral interactions. In actuality, leadership initiative usually begins with the skillful chief executive and is directed at the board. The executive-activated board is critical to the success of the nonprofit organization and the public functions it serves.

If it is true that some executives believe in a much more simple and linear view of the world of nonprofit organizations than do others, what are the implications? An executive with whom we worked from an agency for the homeless answers the question this way: "For too long I assumed that good things would happen to our agency because I thought our agency did good things. Every day I came to work and saw the value of the work we were doing and the needs we were serving. I could not believe that others could not buy into the goodness of our cause. Yet our budget decreased yearly even as demands for our service increased; we almost went out of business. I kept wondering why, with the growing dimensions of the needs we served, our agency's needs were not obvious to everyone else."

Nonprofit organizations like this one do good only if they have the resources to do so. The belief in the effects of good intentions can be blinding. Only when this executive was able to convince her board to find money for a major new fund-raising effort was the agency able to eliminate its deficit. The new allocation for the fund-raising program was a risky one for the board to take. The board had never endorsed aggressive fund raising. It had been conditioned by a kind of dependency — the executive termed it a "welfare mentality" — characteristic of those it served, who waited for others to help them rather than helping themselves.

The allocation was risky for other reasons as well. The staff had not had a pay raise for years. Some staff salaries were close to poverty guidelines. The executive was asking for money for an unproven fund-raising campaign when debts were outstanding and pressure was mounting by some vendors to pay long-overdue bills. Yet the board consented. A $17,000 investment returned $300,000, and the organization was able to do more than simply survive — over the next few years it grew significantly and established a sizable contingency fund.

Every community in America has a group of nonprofit chief executives whose thinking, orientation, and actions are similar to the executive of the homeless program. They have learned how to resolve the seeming contradictions between the traditional (board-driven) view of leadership and the executive-initiated model of leadership advocated by this book. Circumstances drove the executive in the example above to think in new and different ways and to depart radically from prior conceptions of her relationship to the board and prior ways of doing business. There are other executives who regularly engage in these kinds of actions. We find them at the helm of the most successful nonprofit organizations in our community. They are willing to probe beyond the normal boundaries of their organizations; they understand the important responsibility they bear in helping their boards perform their vital roles, and they understand the importance of taking the risks necessary to influence their organization's dependence on environmentally derived resources. They do not see themselves as passive agents compliantly waiting for others to decide what to do, nor have they resigned themselves to accept only those resources that may flow to their organizations in the normal course of events. These are the executives who have discovered that few activities in human endeavor are more fascinating, more challenging, and more rewarding than leading a nonprofit organization with an important mission. They have also discovered that it is their special kind of leadership that is essential to the accomplishment of the critically important goals of the nonprofit sector in our society.

RESOURCES

Self-Assessment Questionnaires for Clarifying Roles and Responsibilities of Boards and Executives

ଡ଼

The following diagnostic questions are designed to assist a chief executive and board who wish to untangle their shared responsibilities and roles. It may be helpful for the chief executive and individual board members to develop separate sets of answers to these questions prior to sharing them with each other. A chief executive and board president may find the questions helpful in thinking about the special nature of their relationship and may want to explore their answers together independently from the rest of the board.

Responses can be shared in terms of both self-expectations and expectations for others. For example, a chief executive may expect a board to shoulder a certain responsibility that the board assumes is the chief executive's or vice versa. It is also possible for individual board members to differ over expectations about roles and responsibilities. If there are major differences among individual board members, they should be addressed and resolved. Since boards frequently change membership, new board members need to be given an opportunity to address these questions soon after joining the board.

Discussion of expectations, intentions, and responsibilities can do much to bring to an explicit level the assumptions, attitudes, and feelings that exist among members of the organization. It is likely that there will be areas of responsibility that have never previously been clarified. The very process of discussion may go a long way to help sort out the strange loops found in most executive-board relations. Differences that are thought to exist may be discovered to be misunderstandings and easily resolved.

Assistance by an outside consultant or third party may be helpful in some cases to help focus discussions and resolve differences. In all cases, the discussions should take place in the spirit of sharing, understanding, and joint problem solving.

The Traditional Conception of Leadership in Nonprofit Organizations

Some would argue that the principal responsibility for leadership in nonprofit organizations resides with the board. It is the board that must identify the mission of the organization, ensure that effective policies are established, and secure sufficient financial and other resources. From this perspective the board holds the chief executive responsible for the exercise of administrative efficiency and the effective delivery of services. The chief executive is subordinate to the board in all matters of critical concern to the organization.

Think about the nonprofit organization in which you are involved. Do you agree with this conceptualization? How are the major responsibilities for mission definition, policy determination, resource generation, and administration presently delineated?

An Alternative Model of Leadership
in Nonprofit Organizations

This book develops a more complex model of leadership of nonprofit organizations than the traditional one. Leadership is found in the relationship between the executive director and the board. If the leadership of the organization is to be effective, the executive director must assist the board in carrying out its crucial duties and responsibilities. The chief executive is held accountable for the success or failure of the organization. The chief executive shares with the board in specific ways the formulation of mission, the determination of policy, the generation of resources, and administration of the services and programs of the organization. The board's responsibilities are not abrogated by the chief executive. Rather, the chief executive works to ensure that the board will carry out its responsibility.

Think about the nonprofit organization in which you are executive director, staff, or member of the board. Do you agree with this alternative conceptualization?

_____

_____

_____

_____

_____

_____

_____

_____

_____

Regarding the Mission of the Organization

How do you respond to the following questions?

1. What is the role of the board in determining the purpose of the organization and its role in the community? What is the role of the chief executive in this regard? Do the chief executive and board agree about the present statement of mission?

_____

_____

_____

_____

2. About what matters relating to the mission should the chief executive advise the board?

_____

_____

_____

_____

3. What is the role of the board in cultivating opportunities and maintaining relationships with external funders, corporate donors, and important government entities that may affect the mission of the organization? What is the role of the chief executive in this regard?

_____

_____

_____

_____

4. What responsibilities does the chief executive have in probing the environment of the organization for opportunities to advance the organization's interest? What is the role of the board?

_____

_____

_____

_____

5. Are the board and chief executive clear with each other about who is responsible for the boundary-spanning activities of the organization?

_____

_____

_____

_____

6. In what ways do the responsibilities of the chief executive intersect with those of the board in maintaining and enhancing the network of stakeholders for the organization?

_____

_____

_____

_____

Regarding the Policies and the Generation
of Resources for the Organization

How do you respond to the following questions?

1. Who should determine the allocation of resources to programs? What are the responsibilities of the board? What are those of the chief executive?

_____

_____

_____

2. Who should determine the plan for resource distribution and decide about the elimination or creation of new programs and services?

_____

_____

_____

3. What responsibilities has the board for determining where resources are to be found? What is the responsibility of the chief executive?

_____

_____

_____

4. Who determines fund-raising and marketing strategies?

_____

_____

Regarding the Administration and Management
of the Organization

How do you respond to the following questions?
1. What administrative functions should be performed by the board?

_____

_____

2. Over what programs, materials, and human resources should the board preside or have oversight? Which should they review? How often should the reviews occur? In what form?

_____

_____

3. What administrative changes should the board instigate, and under what circumstances?

_____

_____

4. What critical information must the chief executive provide the board, in what format, and how often?

_____

_____

5. Whom should the board hire and fire?

_____

_____

REFERENCES

●○○○●

Argyris, C., and Schön, D. A. *Theory in Practice: Increasing Professional Effectiveness.* San Francisco: Jossey-Bass, 1975.

Rader, B. S. "Keys to Better Hospital Governance Through Better Information." In R. D. Herman and J. Van Til (eds.), *Nonprofit Boards of Directors: Analyses and Applications.* New Brunswick, N.J.: Transaction, 1989.

Bloch, P. *The Empowered Manager.* San Francisco: Jossey-Bass, 1988.

Bryson, J. M. *Strategic Planning for Public and Nonprofit Organizations: A Guide to Strengthening and Sustaining Organizational Achievement.* San Francisco: Jossey-Bass, 1988.

Calhoun, J. A. "Essay: Making Bad Kids Good." *Foundation News,* 1989, *30* (4), 31–34.

Carver, J. "Business Leadership on Nonprofit Boards." Board Monograph Series. National Association of Corporate Directors, a division of American Management Associations, 1980.

Chait, R. P., and Taylor, B. E. "Charting the Territory of Nonprofit Boards." *Harvard Business Review,* 1989, *67* (1), 44–54.

Dollinger, M. J. "Environmental Boundary Spanning and Information Processing Effects on Organizational Performance." *Academy of Management Journal,* 1984, *27* (2), 351–368.

Drucker, P. F. *Management: Tasks, Responsibilities, Practices.* New York: Harper & Row, 1974.

141

Drucker, P. F. "Lessons for Successful Nonprofit Governance." *Nonprofit Management and Leadership,* Vol. 1. San Francisco: Jossey-Bass, 1990.

Elmore, R. F. "Organizational Models of Social Program Implementation." *Public Policy,* 1978, *26* (2), 185–228.

Fink, J. "Community Agency Boards of Directors: Viability and Vestigiality, Substance and Symbol." In R. D. Herman and J. Van Til (eds.), *Nonprofit Boards of Directors: Analyses and Applications.* New Brunswick, N.J.: Transaction, 1989.

Firstenberg, P. B. *Managing for Profit in the Nonprofit World.* New York: Foundation Center, 1986.

Fisher, R., and Ury, W. *Getting to Yes.* New York: Penguin, 1983.

Galaskiewicz, J. *Social Organization of an Urban Grants Economy: A Study of Business Philanthropy and Nonprofit Organizations.* Orlando, Fla.: Academic Press, 1985.

Goettler Associates. *The Role of Trustees in Development: Building an Effective Fund-Raising Board.* Columbus, Ohio: Goettler Associates, 1986.

Gronbjerg, K. "Funding Changes and the Management of Nonprofit Organizations." In *Proceedings of the 1989 Conference of the Association of Voluntary Action Scholars.* Seattle, Washington, 1989.

Heimovics, R. D., and Herman, R. D. "Responsibility for Critical Events in Nonprofit Organizations." *Nonprofit and Voluntary Sector Quarterly,* 1990, *19* (1), 59–72.

Herman, R. D. "Concluding Thoughts on Closing the Board Gap." In R. D. Herman and J. Van Til (eds.), *Nonprofit Boards of Directors: Analyses and Applications.* New Brunswick, N.J.: Transaction, 1989.

Herman, R. D., and Heimovics, R. D. "Effective Managers of Nonprofit Organizations." In *Working Papers for the Spring Research Forum.* Washington, D.C.: Independent Sector, 1987.

Herman, R. D., and Heimovics, R. D. "Nonprofit Chief Executives' Careers and Work." In *Working Papers for the Spring Research Forum.* Washington, D.C.: Independent Sector, 1989.

Herman, R. D., and Heimovics, R. D. "An Investigation of Leadership Skill Differences in Chief Executives of Nonprofit

Organizations." *American Review of Public Administration,* 1990, *20* (2), 107–124.

Herman, R. D., and Tulipana, F. P. "Board-Staff Relations and Perceived Effectiveness in Nonprofit Organizations." *Journal of Voluntary Action Research,* 1985, *14* (4), 48–59.

Hodgkinson, V. A., and Lyman, R. W. (eds.). *The Future of the Nonprofit Sector: Challenges, Changes, and Policy Considerations.* San Francisco: Jossey-Bass, 1989.

Houle, C. O. *Governing Boards.* San Francisco: Jossey-Bass, 1989.

Huff, A. S. "Managerial Implications of the Emerging Paradigm." In Y. S. Lincoln (ed.), *Organizational Theory and Inquiry: The Paradigm Revolution.* Beverly Hills, Calif.: Sage, 1985.

Kotter, J. P. *The General Managers.* New York: Free Press, 1982.

Lawrence, P. R., and Lorsch, J. W. *Organization and Environment.* Boston: Harvard Business School, Division of Research, 1967.

Mathews, D. "The Independent Sector and the Political Responsibilities of the Public." Address delivered at the Spring Research Forum, sponsored by Independent Sector, March 19, 1987.

Middleton, M. "Nonprofit Boards of Directors: Beyond the Governance Function." In W. W. Powell (ed.), *The Nonprofit Sector: A Research Handbook.* New Haven, Conn.: Yale University Press, 1987.

Middleton, M. "The Characteristics and Influence of Intraboard Networks: A Case Study of a Nonprofit Board of Directors." In R. D. Herman and J. Van Til (eds.), *Nonprofit Boards of Directors: Analyses and Applications.* New Brunswick, N.J.: Transaction, 1989.

Mintzberg, H. *The Nature of Managerial Work.* New York: Harper & Row, 1973.

Mintzberg, H. "The Manager's Job: Folklore and Fact." *Harvard Business Review,* 1975, *53* (4), 49–61.

Morgan, G. *Images of Organization.* Beverly Hills, Calif.: Sage, 1986.

Nielsen, W. A. *The Endangered Sector.* New York: Columbia University Press, 1979.

O'Connell, B. *The Board Member's Book.* New York: Foundation Center, 1985.

Odendahl, T. J. (ed.). *America's Wealthy and the Future of Foundations.* New York: Foundation Center, 1987.

O'Neill, M. *The Third America: The Emergence of the Nonprofit Sector in the United States.* San Francisco, Calif.: Jossey-Bass, 1989.

Perrow, C. *Complex Organizations: A Critical Essay.* (3rd ed.) New York: Random House, 1986.

Pfeffer, J. *Power in Organizations.* Marshfield, Mass.: Pittman, 1981.

Pfeffer, J. *Organizations and Organization Theory.* Boston: Pitman, 1982.

Powell, W. W. (ed.). *The Nonprofit Sector: A Research Handbook.* New Haven, Conn.: Yale University Press, 1987.

Robbins, S. P. *Managing Organizational Conflict: A Nontraditional Approach.* Englewood Cliffs, N.J.: Prentice-Hall, 1974.

Roethelisberger, F. J. *Man in Organization: Essays of F. J. Roethelisberger.* Cambridge, Mass.: Belknap Press of Harvard University, 1968.

Salamon, L. M. "Partners in Public Service: The Scope and Theory of Government-Nonprofit Relations." In W. W. Powell (ed.), *The Nonprofit Sector: A Research Handbook.* New Haven, Conn.: Yale University Press, 1987.

Salamon, L. M., and Abramson, A. J. *Nonprofit Organizations and the FY 1989 Federal Budget.* Washington, D.C.: Independent Sector, 1988.

Salamon, L. M., Musselwhite, J. C., and DeVita, C. J. "Partners in Public Service: Government and the Nonprofit Sector in the Welfare State." In *Working Papers for the Spring Research Forum.* Washington, D.C.: Independent Sector, 1986.

Simon, J. G. "The Tax Treatment of Nonprofit Organizations: A Review of Federal and State Policies." In W. W. Powell (ed.), *The Nonprofit Sector: A Research Handbook.* New Haven, Conn.: Yale University Press, 1987.

Smith, R. S. "The Politics of Nonprofit Entrepreneurship: the Reagan Era and Beyond." In *Working Papers for the Spring Research Forum.* Washington, D.C.: Independent Sector, 1989.

Terry, R. W. "The Negative Impact on White Values." In B.
  P. Bowser and R. C. Hunt (eds.), *Impacts of Racism on White
  Americans*. Beverly Hills, Calif.: Sage, 1981.
Thibaut, J. W., and Kelley, H. H. *The Social Psychology of Groups*.
  New York: Wiley, 1959.
Van Til, J. *Mapping the Third Sector: Voluntarism in a Changing
  Social Economy*. New York: Foundation Center, 1988.
Weick, K. E. *The Social Psychology of Organizing*. Reading, Mass.:
  Addison-Wesley, 1969.
Widmer, C. "Why Board Members Participate." In R. D. Her-
  man and J. Van Til (eds.), *Nonprofit Boards of Directors: Anal-
  yses and Applications*. New Brunswick, N.J.: Transaction, 1989.
Young, D. R. *Casebook of Management for Non-Profit Organizations*.
  New York: Haworth Press, 1985.
Young, D. R. "Executive Leadership in Nonprofit Organiza-
  tions." In W. W. Powell (ed.), *The Nonprofit Sector: A Research
  Handbook*. New Haven, Conn.: Yale University Press, 1987.
Zald, M. N. "Who Shall Rule? A Political Analysis of Succes-
  sion in a Large Welfare Organization." *Pacific Sociological
  Review*, 1965, *8* (1), 52–60.

INDEX

○○

147